Babies &
Toddlers
-a Knitter's dozen

Babies & Toddlers; A Knitter's dozen PUBLISHED BY XRX BOOKS

Credits

PUBLISHER
Alexis Yiorgos Xenakis

COEDITORS
Rick Mondragon
Elaine Rowley

EDITORIAL COORDINATOR
Sue Kay Nelson

INSTRUCTION EDITOR
Joni Coniglio

INSTRUCTION ASSISTANTS
MaryLou Eastman
Kelly Rokke
Carol Thompson
Lizbeth Upitis

GRAPHIC DESIGNER
Bob Natz

PHOTOGRAPHER
Alexis Xenakis

DIRECTOR, PUBLISHING
SERVICES
David Xenakis

CHIEF EXECUTIVE OFFICER
Benjamin Levisay

STYLIST
Lisa Mannes

TECHNICAL ILLUSTRATOR
Carol Skallerud

PRODUCTION DIRECTOR &
COLOR SPECIALIST
Dennis Pearson

BOOK PRODUCTION MANAGER
Greg Hoogeveen

DIGITAL PREPRESS
Everett Baker
Nancy Holzer
Jay Reeve

MIS
Jason Bittner

FIRST PUBLISHED IN USA IN 2007 BY XRX, INC.

COPYRIGHT © 2007 XRX, INC.

ISBN 10: 1-933064-06-4
ISBN 13: 978-1-933064-06-2

Produced in Sioux Falls, South Dakota, by XRX, Inc.,
PO Box 1525, Sioux Falls, SD 57101-1525 USA 605.338.2450

a publication of **XRX BOOKS**
Visit us online at www.knittinguniverse.com

XRX BOOKS

photography by
Alexis Xenakis

Babies&Toddlers
-a Knitter's dozen

1a

Mrs. Beetle

1b

Mr. Bumble

2

Children
at Play

3

Baby
Delight

4

Mexicali
Baby Ole'

5

3 Speedy
Cardies

6

Heart
Pockets

BLANKETS, CARDIES, SWEATERS, HATS,
SOCKS, ACCESSORIES & TOYS

13a&b

Stitch Heirs

14

Baby
Bunting

15

Amish Baby
Stockings

16

Playful Pairs

17

Bonnie
Bonnet

18a

Baby Blocks
Afghan

18b

Felted Baby
Blocks

CONTENTS

Techniques page 110

1 2 **3** 4 5 6

Specifications page 118

Welcome

The first gift we knit a baby is a welcome—to a world we can shape and make warm, soft, and colorful.

Whether it's hearts or elephants, sunflowers or bugs, stripes or blocks— we bring bits of the world into the shapes we knit. As babies and toddlers wear, curl up in, and play with them, their world grows. And as we knit, so does ours.

We share a growing confidence as we try double knit, entrelac, lace, felting, stranded color and intarsia, socks and shaped-leg stockings— you'll find them all here.

We share a delight in discovery as what we knit surprises us. We watch a hexagon turn into a 4-tam pram set (page 35) or an origami bear take shape (page 91).

We share a sense of security as we recreate a familiar, well-loved knit— a sweater (say the Baby Ole', page 17) or a blanket to grow up with (Children at Play, page 9)—over and over.

Soon your knitter's dozen, like ours, will grow to two dozen . . . or more.

Throughout this book, the yarns are described generically and the specific yarn is listed with each photograph. Some of the yarns are no longer available, but may live on in our memories and stashes.

Designed by Lorna Miser

1a

Mrs. Beetle

LOOSE FIT

CARDIGAN
6 (12, 24) months
A 22 (24½, 26¾)"
B 10 (11, 12½)"
C 12 (14½, 17)"

HAT
Circumference 14 (16, 18)"

10cm/4"

19/20

13/14

• over stockinette stitch (knit on RS, purl on WS), using larger (smaller) needles

1 2 3 4 **5** 6

• Bulky weight
CARDIGAN
MC • 135 (175, 235) yds
A • 50 (60, 65) yds
B • 30 (40, 60) yds
HAT
MC • 20 (20, 25) yds
A • 40 (50, 70) yds

• 5.5mm/US 9 and 6mm/US 10, or size to obtain gauge, 60cm/24" long
• 5.5mm/US 9, 40cm/16" long

Notes
1 See *Techniques*, page 110, for SSK, yarn over (yo), 3-needle bind-off, slip stitch crochet, crochet chain stitch, and chain stitch embroidery. **2** Body of sweater is worked in one piece to underarm, then divided and fronts and back are worked separately.

Stripe Pattern
With A, knit 4 rows, with MC, [knit 1 row, purl 1 row] twice, with B, knit 4 rows, with MC, [knit 1 row, purl 1 row] twice; repeat from (16 rows) for Stripe Pattern.

Decrease Rows
At beginning of RS rows K1, SSK.
At end of RS rows K2tog, k1.

CARDIGAN
Body
With smaller needle and B, cast on 68 (76, 84) stitches. Knit 6 rows. Change to larger needle. With MC, work in stockinette stitch for 22 (26, 26)

four 5.5mm/US 9

5.5mm/I-9

• three 19mm/¾"

&

• stitch markers (stitch markers) and holders
• yarn needle

rows. Piece measures approximately 5½ (6½, 6½)" from beginning.
Divide for fronts and back
Begin Stripe Pattern: Next row (RS) With A, k17 (19, 21) (for right front) and place these stitches on hold, k34 (38, 42) (for back) and place these stitches on hold, knit to end (for left front).
Next row (WS) Knit 17 (19, 21) stitches of left front.

Left Front
Shape V-neck
Continue in Stripe Pattern, AT SAME TIME, decrease 1 stitch at neck edge (end of RS rows) on next row, then every other row 6 times more, then every 4th row 0 (0, 2) times—10 (12, 12) stitches. Work 9 rows even, ending with 4 rows MC. Armhole measures approximately 4½ (4½, 6)". Place stitches on hold.

Right Front
Next row (WS) Join A and knit 1 row. Work to correspond to left front, reversing neck shaping by working decreases at beginning of RS rows.

Back
Next row (WS) Join A and knit 1 row. Continue in Stripe Pattern until armhole

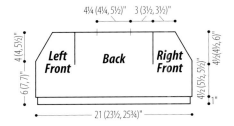

4¼ (4¼, 5½)" 3 (3½, 3½)"

4 (4, 5½)"

6 (7, 7)"

Left Front **Back** **Right Front**

4½ (5½)", 6"

4½ (5½)", 6"

4½ (5½, 5½)"

1"

21 (23½, 25¾)"

9 (9, 12)"

¾"

Sleeve

5½ (7, 9)"

¾"

6½ (7, 7¾)"

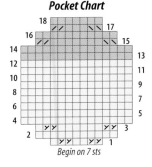

Pocket Chart

Begin on 7 sts

Stitch Key

☐ Knit on RS, purl on WS
◣ SSK
◪ K2tog
◪ Knit into front and back of stitch

Color Key

▨ MC
☐ A or B

measures same length as fronts. Place stitches on hold.

Sleeves

With smaller needle and B, cast on 21 (23, 25) stitches. Knit 4 rows. Change to larger needle. With MC, work in stockinette stitch, increasing 1 stitch each side on 5th (11th, 5th) row, then every 6th (10th, 6th) row 3 (2, 6) times more—29 (29, 39) stitches. Work 3 (3, 1) rows even. Piece measures approximately 6¼ (7¾, 9¾)" from beginning. With A, knit 4 rows. Bind off.

Right Front Pocket

With larger needle and A, cast on 7 stitches. Work 18 rows of Pocket Chart. Bind off. With yarn needle and MC, work straight stitch down center of A section of pocket and work 3 French knots on each side.

Left Front Pocket

Work as for right front pocket, using B instead of A.

Finishing

Block pieces.
Join shoulders, using 3-needle bind-off, as follows: Join 10 (12, 12) stitches of first shoulder, then bind off neck stitches until 10 (12, 12) stitches remain for 2nd shoulder, join remaining stitches. Sew sleeves into armholes. Sew sleeve seams. Sew pockets on front, using photo as guide.

Front and neckband

Place 3 markers for buttonholes along right front edge, with the first ½" from lower edge, the last 1½" below first neck decrease, and 1 centered between. With RS facing, smaller needle and A, begin at lower edge and pick up and knit 34 (38, 44) stitches along right front edge, 14 (14, 18) stitches along back neck, and 34 (38, 44) stitches along left front edge—82 (90, 106) stitches. Knit 5 rows, working buttonholes (by yo, k2tog) at markers on 2nd row. Bind off. Sew on buttons.

Your little one will be all the buzz in this charming cardigan and hat.

Designed by Lorna Miser

Mr. Bumble

EASY

STANDARD FIT
CARDIGAN
6 (12, 24) months
A 19¾ (20¾, 22¾)"
B 9½ (10½, 12)"
C 12 (12, 17½)"
HAT
Circumference 14½ (16, 17¼)"

10cm/4"

26/26
18/18

• over stockinette stitch
(knit on RS, purl on WS)

1 2 3 **4** 5 6

• Medium weight
CARDIGAN
MC • 170 (195, 280) yds
CC • 110 (115, 175) yds
HAT
MC • 30 (30, 35) yds
CC • 55 (60, 65) yds

• 4.5mm/US 7, or size to obtain gauge,
60cm/24" long
40cm/16" long for hat

• four 4.5mm/US 7

Notes

1 See *Techniques*, page 110, for SSK, and 3-needle bind-off. **2** Body of sweater is worked in one piece to underarm, then divided and fronts and back are worked separately.

Stripe Pattern

Work in stockinette stitch as follows: *4 rows CC, 4 rows MC; repeat from* for Stripe Pattern.

Decrease Rows

At beginning of RS rows K1, SSK.
At end of RS rows K2tog, k1.

Body

With CC, cast on 77 (81, 89) stitches. Work in k1, p1 rib for 4 rows, increasing 9 (9, 10) stitches evenly across last row—86 (90, 99) stitches. With MC, work in stockinette stitch for 28 (34, 36) rows. Piece measures approximately 5 (6, 6¼)" from beginning.

Divide for fronts and back

Next row (RS) K21 (22, 24) (for right front) and place these stitches on hold,

k44 (46, 51) (for back) and place these stitches on hold, knit to end (for left front). **Next row** (WS) Purl 21 (22, 24) stitches of left front.

Left Front

Shape V-neck

Work in Stripe Pattern, AT SAME TIME, decrease 1 stitch at neck edge (end of RS rows) on 3rd row, then every other row 6 (6, 4) times more, then every 4th row 2 (2, 5) times—12 (13, 14) stitches. Work 5 rows even, ending with 4 rows CC. Armhole measures approximately 4½ (4½, 5¾)". Place stitches on hold.

Right Front

Next row (WS) Join MC and purl 1 row. Work to correspond to left front, reversing neck shaping by working decreases at beginning of RS rows.

Back

Next row (WS) Join MC and purl 1 row. Work in Stripe Pattern until armhole measures same length as fronts. Place stitches on hold.

• four 19mm/¾"

• stitch markers (stitch markers) and holders
• yarn needle

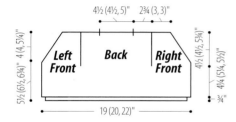

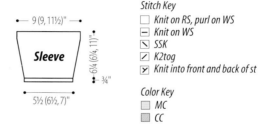

Pocket Chart

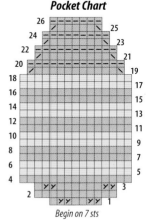

Begin on 7 sts

Sleeves

With CC, cast on 25 (29, 31) stitches. Work in k1, p1 rib for 4 rows. Work in stockinette stitch as follows: Work 4 rows with MC, then work in Stripe Pattern, AT SAME TIME, increase 1 stitch each side on 5th (5th, 7th) row, then every 4th (6th, 6th) row 6 (5, 6) times, then every 6th (0, 8th) row 1 (0, 3) times—41 (41, 51) stitches. Work 5 rows even, ending with 4 rows CC. Piece measures approximately 7 (7, 11¾)" from beginning. Bind off.

Pockets (make 2)

With CC, cast on 7 stitches. Work 26 rows of Pocket Chart. Bind off.

Finishing

Block pieces.

Join shoulders, using 3-needle bind-off, as follows: Join 12 (13, 14) stitches of first shoulder, bind off back neck stitches until 12 (13, 14) stitches remain for 2nd shoulder, join remaining stitches. Sew sleeves into armholes. Sew sleeve seams. Sew pockets on front, using photo as guide. With CC, embroider wings using straight stitch.

Front and neck band

Place 4 markers for buttonholes along left front edge, with the first ½" from lower edge, the last 1" below first neck decrease, and 2 others spaced evenly between. With RS facing and CC, begin at lower edge and pick up and knit 50 (54, 64) stitches along right front edge, 19 (19, 23) stitches along back neck, and 50 (54, 64) stitches along left front edge—119 (127, 151) stitches. Work in k1, p1 rib for 4 rows, working buttonholes (by yo, k2tog) at markers on 2nd row. Bind off. Sew on buttons.

MRS. BEETLE HAT

With circular needle and A, cast on 50 (56, 64) stitches. Place marker, join and work in k1, p1 rib for 4 rounds, decreasing 1 (0, 1) stitch on last round—49 (56, 63) stitches. Knit 12 (14, 17) rounds.

Shape crown

Note Change to double-pointed needles when necessary.

Next round [K5, k2tog] 7 (8, 9) times. Knit 1 round.

Next round [K4, k2tog] 7 (8, 9) times. Change to MC. Knit 1 round.

Next round [K3, k2tog] 7 (8, 9) times. Knit 1 round.

Next round [K2, k2tog] 7 (8, 9) times. Knit 1 round.

Next round [K1, k2tog] 7 (8, 9) times. Knit 1 round.

Next round [K2tog] 7 (8, 9) times. Cut yarn, draw through remaining 7 (8, 9) stitches and pull together. Secure yarn to WS.

Antennae

With crochet hook and MC, join yarn at top of hat and *chain 15, turn and work slip stitch in each chain; repeat from* once more for 2nd antenna.

Embroidery

With MC, embroider line down each side of hat using chain stitch. Work 3 French knots on each side.

MR. BUMBLE HAT

With CC, cast on 60 (64, 70) stitches. Place marker, join and work in k1, p1 rib for 4 rounds, increasing 6 (8, 8) stitches evenly around on last round—66 (72, 78) stitches. Knit 4 rounds with MC, then work in Stripe Pattern for 18 rounds, ending with 2 rounds CC. Hat measures approximately 4¼" from beginning. Cut MC.

Shape crown

Note Change to double-pointed needles when necessary. With CC, work as follows:

Size 24 months only: Next round [K11, k2tog] 6 times. Knit 1 round.

Sizes 12 (24) months only: Next round [K10, k2tog] 6 times. Knit 1 round.

All Sizes: Next round [K9, k2tog] 6 times. Knit 1 round.

Next round [K8, k2tog] 6 times. Knit 1 round.

Next round [K7, k2tog] 6 times. Knit 1 round.

Next round [K6, k2tog] 6 times. Knit 1 round.

Next round [K5, k2tog] 6 times. Knit 1 round.

Next round [K4, k2tog] 6 times. Knit 1 round.

Next round [K3, k2tog] 6 times—24 stitches.

Next round [K2tog] 12 times.

Next round [K2tog] 6 times. Cut yarn, draw through remaining 6 stitches and pull together. Secure yarn to WS.

2

Like child's play, this afghan mixes double and single mitered squares.
The colors will charm the little prince or princess in your life.

Designed by Shawn Stoner

Children At Play

INTERMEDIATE

One size

50" x 41"

10cm/4"

35

18

• over Garter Ridge Pattern

1 2 3 **4** 5 6

• Medium weight
  • A 1,000 yds
  • B 1,200 yds
  • C 1,000 yds

• 4mm/US 6,
or size to obtain gauge

&

• stitch markers

Notes

1 See *Techniques*, page 110, for SSK, cable cast-on, invisible cast-on, pick up and knit, and grafting. **2** Use cable cast-on throughout except when casting on for border. **3** Stitches for squares and rectangles are obtained by either casting on or picking up stitches. Refer to text and diagram for where to cast on or pick up stitches. **4** Pick up stitches with RS of work facing.

Garter Ridge Pattern (For gauge swatch)
Rows 1 and 3 (RS) Knit.
Row 2 Purl.
Row 4 (WS) Knit.
Repeat rows 1–4 for Garter Ridge Pattern.

27
27

Large Square (Over 54 stitches)
Foundation row (WS) K27, place marker (pm), k27.
Rows 1 and 3 (RS) Knit to 2 stitches before marker, k2tog, slip marker (sm), SSK, knit to end.
Row 2 Purl.
Row 4 Knit.
Repeat Rows 1–4 eleven times more, then repeat Rows 1 and 2 once more.
Next row (RS) K2tog, SSK—2 stitches. Bind off.

13 13

Small Square (Over 26 stitches)
Foundation row (WS) K13, pm, k13.
Rows 1 and 3 (RS) Knit to 2 stitches before marker, k2tog, sm, SSK, knit to end.
Row 2 Purl.
Row 4 Knit.
Repeat Rows 1–4 four times more, then repeat Rows 1 and 2 once more.
Next row (RS) K2tog, SSK—2 stitches. Bind off.

13 26 13

Rectangle (Over 52 stitches)
Foundation row (WS) K13, pm, k26, pm, k13.
Rows 1 and 3 (RS) [Knit to 2 stitches before marker, k2tog, sm, SSK] twice, knit to end.
Row 2 Purl.
Row 4 Knit.
Repeat Rows 1–4 four times more, then repeat Rows 1 and 2 once more.
Next row (RS) [K2tog, SSK] twice—4 stitches. Bind off.

AFGHAN

Block 1 With A, cast on 54 stitches. Work Large Square.
Blocks 2 and 3 With B, pick up and knit 27 stitches along top edge of preceding block, cast on 27 stitches. Work Large Square.

10

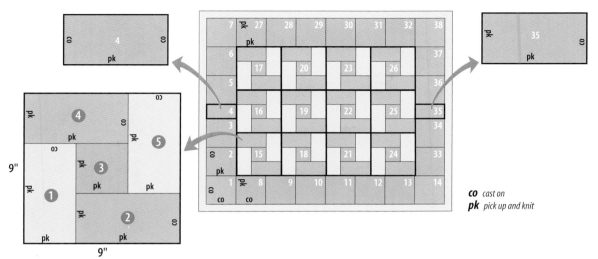

co *cast on*
pk *pick up and knit*

Block 4 With B, cast on 13 stitches, pick up and knit 26 stitches along top of Block 3, cast on 13 stitches. Work Rectangle.

Blocks 5 and 6 Work as for Block 2.

Block 7 With A, work as for Block 2.

Block 8 With B, cast on 27 stitches, pick up and knit 27 stitches along right side of Block 1. Work Large Square.

Blocks 9–13 Work as for Block 8.

Block 14 With A, work as for Block 8.

Block 15 With C, pick up and knit 13 stitches along left half of top edge of Block 8 and 26 stitches along right edge of Block 2, cast on 13 stitches. Work Rectangle.

With A, cast on 13 stitches, pick up and knit 13 stitches along left half of top edge of Block 9 and 13 stitches along right half of top edge of Block 8, pick up and knit 13 stitches along lower half of C rectangle. Work Rectangle.

With B, pick up and knit 13 stitches along left half of top edge of A rectangle and 13 stitches along top half of C rectangle. Work Small Square.

With A, cast on 13 stitches, pick up and knit 13 stitches along top edge of B square and 13 stitches along top edge of C rectangle, pick up and knit 13 stitches along lower half of Block 3. Work Rectangle.

With C, pick up and knit 13 stitches along right half of A rectangle, 13 stitches along B square, and 13 stitches along A rectangle, cast on 13 stitches. Work Rectangle.

Blocks 16–26 Work as for Block 15, casting on and picking up stitches as indicated in diagram.

Block 27 With B, pick up and knit 27 stitches along top of A rectangle from Block 17 and 27 stitches along right edge of Block 7. Work Large Square.

Blocks 28–34 Work as for Block 27, picking up stitches as indicated in diagram.

Block 35 With B, cast on 13 stitches, pick up and knit 26 stitches along top edge of Block 34 and 13 stitches along half of C rectangle from Block 25. Work Rectangle.

Blocks 36 and 37 Work as for Block 27.

Block 38 With A, work as for Block 27.

Finishing
BORDER

Note Begin border at center of a side edge.

With C, invisibly cast on 6 stitches.

* ***Row 1*** (RS) K6, then pick up and knit 1 stitch from edge of afghan, turn.

Row 2 (WS) P2tog, p5.

Row 3 Repeat Row 1.

Row 4 K2tog, k5.

Repeat Rows 1–4 to corner, ending with Row 4.

Work corner: Row 1 (RS) K5, turn work.

Row 2 and all WS rows Knit to end of row.

Row 3 K4, turn.

Row 5 K3, turn.

Row 7 K2, turn.

Row 9 K1, turn.

Row 11 K2, turn.

Row 13 K3, turn.

Row 15 K4, turn.

Row 17 K5, turn.

Knit to end. Repeat from* around entire afghan (picking up first stitch in corner stitch).

Graft stitches together at side edge.

GO TO
knittinguniverse.com
Web Features
Knitter's Paintbox
to try your own colors.

3

Here's a jacket and hat set to make for all your expectant friends and relatives. Size the pattern up by changing the yarn weight and gauge. We've given the pattern for a size 3 months, using a light weight yarn. Our 18-month version was knit with a medium weight yarn and size 5mm/US 8 needles. The top-down construction makes it easy to adjust lengths.

Designed by Irene Kubilius

Baby Delight

INTERMEDIATE

B ──┤ **A**

C

STANDARD FIT

CARDIGAN
3 months
A 18"
B 10¼"
C 11¼"

BONNET
Width 12¾"
Length 7¾"

10cm/4"

30 ▦ 22

• over stockinette stitch
(knit on RS, purl on WS)

1 2 **3** 4 5 6

• Light weight
Cardigan and bonnet
475 yards

• 4mm/US 6,
or size to obtain gauge

• 4mm/US 6, 40cm/16" long

• 4mm/G

• four 13mm/½"

&

• stitch markers

Notes
1 See *Techniques*, page 110, for SSK, yarn over (yo), and crochet chain.
2 Cardigan is worked from the top down. **3** After first buttonhole, work buttonhole every 10th garter ridge 3 times more.

CARDIGAN
Collar
With straight needles, cast on 52 stitches. Work in garter stitch (knit every row) for 24 rows (12 garter ridges).
Next (decrease) row (WS) K4, [p2tog] 22 times, k4—30 stitches.

Next row Knit.
Next row K4, p22, k4.
Next row K4, [knit into front and back of next stitch] 22 times, k4—52 stitches.
Next row K4, p44, k4.
Begin Chart Patterns: Row 1 (RS) Work Left Front Chart over 10 stitches, place marker (pm), work Sleeve Chart over 8 stitches, pm, work Back Chart over 16 stitches, pm, work Sleeve Chart over 8 stitches, pm, work Right Front Chart over 10 stitches—60 stitches. Continue in patterns as established through chart row 32. Change to circular needle. Work chart rows 33 and

Right Front Chart ———— **Sleeve Chart**

10 sts to 27 sts   8 sts to 41 sts

14

Page 16 size 18 months PLYMOUTH Encore Colorspun (acrylic, wool; 100g; 200 yds) in blue

34, removing markers on last row.
Divide for body and sleeves
Next row With circular needle, work 27 stitches of left front as follows: k5, pm, work 7 stitches of Gull Wing Chart, pm, k15; with straight needles, work 41 stitches of left sleeve as follows: k17, pm, work 7 stitches of Gull Wing Chart, pm, k17. Continue working sleeve stitches only as follows:

Left Sleeve

Continue working Gull Wing Chart between markers and remaining stitches in stockinette stitch, AT SAME TIME, decrease 1 stitch each side every 6th row 5 times—31 stitches. Knit 9 rows (removing markers). Bind off all stitches purlwise.

With circular needle, work across 49 stitches of back as follows: k21, pm, work 7 stitches of Gull Wing Chart, pm, k21; with straight needles, work 41 stitches of right sleeve as for left sleeve. With circular needle, work across 27

stitches of right front as follows: k15, pm, work 7 stitches of Gull Wing Chart, pm, k5—103 stitches on circular needle for body.

Body

Next row (WS) K4, p1, work 7 stitches of Gull Wing Chart, [p36, work 7 stitches of Gull Wing Chart] twice, p1, k4. Continue in pattern as established (working 2 more buttonholes after every 10th ridge as established on right front edge) until body measures approximately 5¼" from underarm, end with row 3 of Gull Wing Chart. Knit 5 rows. Bind off all stitches purlwise.

Finishing

Block cardigan. Sew sleeve seams. Sew buttons on left front.

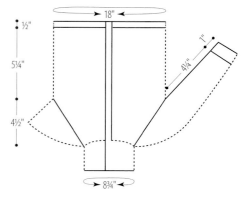

Gull Wing Chart

7 sts

Stitch Key

☐ Knit on RS, purl on WS
▨ Knit on WS
⊡ Yo
⟋ K2tog
⟍ SSK

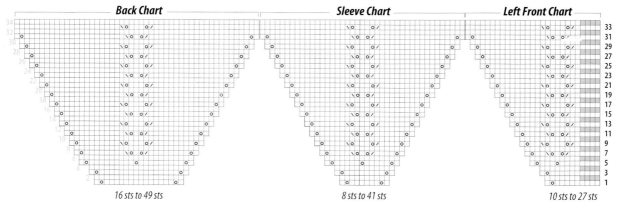

Back Chart	Sleeve Chart	Left Front Chart
16 sts to 49 sts	8 sts to 41 sts	10 sts to 27 sts

BONNET

Cast on 9 stitches, leaving a 10" tail. Purl 1 row on WS.

Shape crown

Row 1 (RS) K1, [yo, k1] 8 times—17 stitches.

Row 2 and all WS rows Purl.

Row 3 K1, [yo, k2] 8 times.

Row 5 K1, [yo, k3] 8 times.

Row 7 K1, [yo, k4] 8 times.

Row 9 K1, [yo, k5] 8 times.

Row 11 K1, [yo, k6] 8 times.

Row 13 K1, [yo, k7] 8 times—65 stitches.

Rows 15, 17, and 19 Knit.

Row 21 [K16, yo] 3 times, k17—68 stitches.

Begin Gull Wing Chart: Row 1 (RS) K13, [pm, work Gull Wing Chart over 7 stitches, pm, k10] twice, pm, work Gull Wing Chart over 7 stitches, pm, k14. Continue in pattern as established until 4 rows of chart have been worked 7 times, work rows 1–3 once more. Knit 5 rows. Bind off stitches purlwise. With yarn from cast-on, sew crown seam for 2½".

Edgings

With RS facing, pick up and knit 25 stitches along each remaining side of seam—50 stitches. Knit 2 rows. Bind off all stitches knitwise on WS.

Ties (make 2)

With crochet hook, loosely chain 56 stitches. Fasten off. Sew one tie to each side of bonnet.

Size 3 months PLYMOUTH Magic Toy Box Collection Pippi (acrylic, nylon, polyester; 50g; 159 yds) in Lavender

Mexicali
Baby Olé

Quick to knit in a colorful, self-patterning yarn, this stylish sweater set would be welcomed by any new mom.

Designed by Mary Gildersleeve

Mexicali Baby Olé

INTERMEDIATE

OVERSIZED FIT
6 (12, 18) months

SWEATER
A 22 (24, 26)"
B 9½ (10½, 11½)"
C 10½ (11½, 12½)"

HAT
Circumference 14½ (18, 18½)"

10cm/4"
34
24

• over stockinette stitch
(knit on RS, purl on WS)

1 **2** 3 4 5 6

• Fine weight
• 459 (550, 650) yds for both

• 3.5mm/US 4, 40cm/16" long

• 3.5mm/US 4 for hat

&

• stitch holders for sweater
• stitch markers for hat

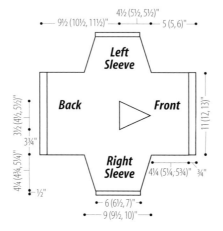

Notes

1 See *Techniques*, page 110, for cable cast-on, wrapping stitches on short rows, and I-cord. **2** Sweater is knit from wrist to wrist in one piece. **3** Use cable cast-on throughout.

SWEATER

Body

Right sleeve

Cast on 36 (40, 42) stitches. Knit 4 rows. Work in stockinette stitch, increasing 1 stitch each side on next row, then every 4th row 8 (6, 4) times, every 6th row 0 (2, 4) times—54 (58, 60) stitches. Work 4 rows even, ending with a RS row. Piece measures approximately 4¾ (5¼, 5¾)" from beginning.

Front and back

Next row (WS) Purl to end, cast on 30 (35, 39) stitches (for front).

Next row (WS) Knit to end, then cast on 30 (35, 39) stitches (for back)—114 (128, 138) stitches.

Next row (WS) K4, purl to last 4 stitches, k4.

Next row Knit.

Repeat last 2 rows 13 times more.

Next row Knit. Shoulder measures approximately 3¾".

Divide for front and back

Next row (RS) K57 (64, 69) front stitches and place remaining stitches on hold.

Shape front neck

Bind off at beginning of every WS row 2 stitches 1 (1, 3) times, 3 stitches 3 (5, 9) times, 4 stitches 4 (4, 0) times—30 (31, 36) stitches.

Cast on at end of every RS row 4 stitches 4 (4, 0) times, 3 stitches 3 (5, 9) times, 2 stitches 1 (1, 3) times—57 (64, 69) stitches. Place stitches on hold.

18

Page 17 Size 6 months FORTISSIMA Colori 1000 (wool, polyester; 100g; 459 yds) in Mexiko

Back

Place stitches from back holder on needle, ready to work a RS row. Work 31 (39, 47) rows even.

Join front and back

Next row (WS) Purl to end of back stitches, then purl stitches from front holder—114 (128, 138) stitches. Work 30 rows even.

Next row (RS) Bind off 30 (35, 39) stitches, knit to end.

Next row (WS) Bind off 30 (35, 39) stitches, purl to end—54 (58, 60) stitches.

Left sleeve

Work 2 rows even. Decrease 1 stitch each side on next row, then every 6th row 0 (2, 4) times, then every 4th row 8 (6, 4) times—36 (40, 42) stitches. Knit 4 rows. Bind off.

Finishing

Block piece. Sew side and sleeve seams.

Collar

Note RS of collar faces WS of sweater.

With RS of sweater facing, begin at center of V-neck and pick up and knit 26 (32, 32) stitches along right front neck, 30 (38, 46) stitches along back neck, and 26 (32, 32) stitches along left front neck—82 (102, 110) stitches. Break yarn. Turn work.

Begin short-row shaping: Row 1 (RS of collar) Slip first 23 (29, 29) stitches to right needle, rejoin yarn, k36 (44, 52), wrap next stitch and turn (W&T).

Row 2 P36 (44, 52), W&T.

Row 3 K36 (44, 52), knit next stitch and wrap together, hiding wrap (HKW), k1, W&T.

Row 4 P38 (46, 54), purl next stitch and wrap together, hiding wrap (HPW), p1, W&T.

Row 5 Knit to wrapped stitch from preceding knit row, HKW, k1, W&T.

Row 6 Purl to wrapped stitch from preceding purl row, HPW, p1, W&T.

Repeat Rows 5 and 6 nine times more.

Next row Knit to end, hiding last wrap.

Next row Purl to end, hiding last wrap. Knit 3 rows. Bind off knitwise on WS.

HAT

Note Change to double-pointed needles when necessary.

Cast on 88 (108, 112) stitches. Place marker (pm), join and work in stockinette stitch (knit every round) until piece measures approximately 3½ (4, 4)" from beginning (with edge rolled).

Next round [K11 (12, 14), pm] 8 (9, 8) times (using last marker placed as round marker).

Shape crown

Decrease round [Knit to 2 stitches before marker, k2tog] 8 (9, 8) times—80 (99, 104) stitches. Repeat Decrease round every round 4 times more—48 (63, 72) stitches.

*Knit 1 round. Work Decrease round once; repeat from * 2 (3, 4) times more—24 (27, 32) stitches.

*Knit 2 rounds. Work Decrease round once; repeat from *1 (1, 2) times more, removing markers on last round—8 (9, 8) stitches.

Next round [K2tog] 4 times, k0 (0, 1)—4 (5, 4) stitches. Work I-cord for 8 rounds. Knit all stitches together. Fasten off last stitch. Tie cord into a knot.

20

5

3 Speedy
Cardies

5 Flowers

it's easy ...go for it!

EASY

LOOSE FIT

CARDIGAN • 2–4 years
A 27"
B 12"
C 18"

HAT
Circumference 17¼"

10cm/4"

18
12

• over stockinette stitch
(knit on RS, purl on WS)

1 2 3 4 **5** 6

• Bulky weight
A • 250 yds
B, C, D • 100 yds each

• 6mm/US 10, or size to obtain gauge

• five 19mm/¾"

• stitch markers
• tapestry needle

Note

See *Techniques*, page 110, for lazy-daisy stitch, French knot, yarn over (yo), and pompons.

Garter Ridge Pattern

Rows 1, 3 and 5 (RS) Knit.
Rows 2 and 4 Purl.
Row 6 (WS) Knit.
Repeat Rows 1–6 for Garter Ridge Pattern.

Back

With A, cast on 43 stitches. Work in k1, p1 rib for 1½", increasing 1 stitch on last (WS) row—44 stitches. Cut A. *With B, [knit 1 row, purl 1 row] twice. With C, knit 2 rows.* With B, knit 1 row, purl 1 row. With C, knit 2 rows. Repeat from* to* once. With B, [knit 1 row, purl 1 row] twice. Cut B and C.
Next row (RS) With D, knit.
Begin seed stitch: Row 1 (WS) *K1, p1; repeat from*. Repeat Row 1 eleven times more. Cut D.
With A, purl 1 row, knit 2 rows. Work rows 1–6 of Garter Ridge Pattern 3 times. Knit 1 row, purl 1 row. Bind off. Piece measures approximately 12" from beginning.

Right Front

With A, cast on 19 stitches. Work rib as for back, increasing 1 stitch on last (WS) row—20 stitches. Work as for back until piece measures 9½" from beginning, end with a WS row.
Shape neck
Next row (RS) Bind off 4 stitches, work to end. Decrease 1 stitch at beginning of every RS row 4 times—12 stitches. Work even until piece measures same length as back. Bind off.

Left Front

Work as for right front, reversing neck shaping. Bind off for neck at beginning of a WS row. Work neck decreases at end of RS rows.

Sleeves

With C, cast on 25 stitches. Work in k1, p1 rib for 1½", increasing 1 stitch on last (WS) row—26 stitches. Cut C. With MC, work in Garter Ridge Pattern, AT SAME TIME, increase 1 stitch each side (working increases into pattern) on 5th row, then every 4th row twice, then every 6th row 4 times—40 stitches. Work even until piece measures 11" from beginning. Bind off.

PAGE 21 BROWN SHEEP CO. Lamb's Pride Bulky (wool, mohair; 115g; 125yds) in Off-white (A), Teal (B), Pink (C), and Purple (D)

Finishing

Block pieces. Sew shoulders.

Button band

With RS facing and C, pick up and knit 43 stitches evenly along left front edge. Work in k1, p1 rib for 1". Bind off in rib. Place 5 markers along band for buttons, with the first 1" from lower edge, the last ½" from top edge, and 3 others spaced evenly between.

Buttonhole band

Work as for button band, working buttonholes (work 2 together, yo) to correspond to button markers when band measures ½".

Neckband

With RS facing and A, pick up and knit 63 stitches evenly around neck edge. Work in k1, p1 rib for ¾". Bind off in rib. Work embroidery on back and fronts, using photo as guide. Work lazy-daisy stitch with C and French knots with B. Place markers on front and back 6¼" down from shoulders for armhole. Sew top of sleeves between markers. Sew side and sleeve seams. Sew on buttons.

HAT

With C, cast on 53 stitches. Change to D and work in k1, p1 rib for 16 rows, increasing 1 stitch on last (WS) row—54 stitches. *With B, work rows 1–4 of Garter Ridge Pattern, with D, work rows 5 and 6 of pattern; repeat from* 4 times more. Cut D. Continue with B only.

Shape top

Row 1 (RS) [K2tog, k1] 18 times—36 stitches.
Row 2 Purl.
Row 3 [K2tog] 18 times—18 stitches.
Row 4 (WS) [P2tog] 9 times—9 stitches. Break yarn, leaving an 18" tail. Draw yarn through remaining stitches and gather together. Sew side seam. With C, make a pompon and attach to top. Fold rib to RS.

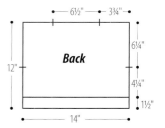

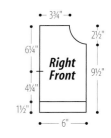

Spots

Note

See *Techniques*, page 110, for French knots.

Garter Ridge Pattern

Rows 1 and 3 (RS) With E, knit.
Rows 2 and 4 With E, purl.
Row 5 With B, knit.
Row 6 (WS) With B, knit. Repeat Rows 1–6 for Garter Ridge Pattern.

Back

With A, cast on 43 stitches. Work in k1, p1 rib for 1½", increasing 1 stitch on last (WS) row—44 stitches. Cut A. *With B, [knit 1 row, purl 1 row] twice. With C, knit 2 rows.* With B, knit 1 row, purl 1 row. With C, knit 2 rows.
Repeat from*to* once. With B, [knit 1 row, purl 1 row] twice.
Next row (RS) With C, knit.
Beginning with a WS row, work Basketweave Chart for 12 rows. Cut C. With D, purl 1 row, knit 2 rows. *[Knit 1 row, purl 1 row] twice. Knit 2 rows. Repeat from* twice more. Knit 1 row, purl 1 row. Bind off. Piece measures approximately 12" from beginning.

Right Front

With A, cast on 19 stitches. Work rib as for back, increasing 1 stitch on last (WS) row—20 stitches. Work as for back until piece measures 9½" from beginning, end with a WS row.

Shape neck

Next row (RS) Bind off 4 stitches, work to end. Decrease 1 stitch at beginning of every RS row 4 times—12 stitches. Work even until piece measures same length as back. Bind off.

Left Front

Work as for right front, reversing neck shaping. Bind off for neck at beginning of a WS row. Work neck decreases at end of RS rows.

Sleeves

With A, cast on 25 stitches. Work in k1, p1 rib for 1½", increasing 1 stitch on last (WS) row—26 stitches. Cut A. Work in Garter Ridge Pattern, AT SAME TIME, increase 1 stitch each side (working increases into pattern) on 5th row, then every 4th row twice, then every 6th row 4 times—40 stitches. Work even until piece measures 11" from beginning. Bind off.

Finishing

Block pieces. Sew shoulders.
Front and neck bands
Using E for all bands, work as for Flowers cardigan working buttonband on right front.
With E, and using photo as guide, work French knots on back and fronts. Place markers on front and back 6¼" down from shoulders for armhole. Sew top of sleeves between markers. Sew side and sleeve seams. Sew on buttons.

Page 25 BROWN SHEEP CO. Lamb's Pride Bulky (wool, mohair; 115g; 125yds) in Light Brown (A), Orange (B), Rust (C), Black (D), and Off-white (E)

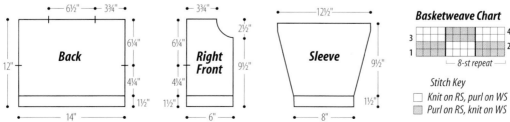

Basketweave Chart

8-st repeat

Stitch Key
☐ Knit on RS, purl on WS
▨ Purl on RS, knit on WS

Back
6½"   3¾"
6¼"
12"
4¼"
1½"
14"

Right Front
3¾"
2½"
6¼"
9½"
4¼"
1½"
6"

Sleeve
12½"
9½"
1½"
8"

Strawberry

Notes

1 See *Techniques*, page 110, for yarn over (yo). **2** Work with 2 strands of yarn held together throughout.

Back

With 2 strands A, cast on 57 stitches. Work in k1, p1 rib for 1", end with a WS row. Work Chart Pattern until piece measures 12½" from beginning. Bind off.

Right Front

With 2 strands A, cast on 33 stitches. Work in k1, p1 rib for 1", increasing 1 stitch at beginning of last (WS) row—34 stitches. **Begin Chart Pattern: Row 1** (RS) Slip first 5 stitches to a holder (for button band), then join 2 strands MC and work row 1 of Chart Pattern over remaining 29 stitches. Work even in pattern until piece measures 10¼" from beginning, end with a WS row.

Shape neck

Next row (RS) Bind off 5 stitches, work to end. Continue to bind off at beginning of every RS row 2 stitches 4 times— 16 stitches. Work even until piece measures same length as back. Bind off.

Left Front

With 2 strands A, cast on 33 stitches. Work in k1, p1 rib for ½", end with a WS row.

Buttonhole row (RS) Work to last 3 stitches, k2tog, yo, k1. Continue in rib pattern for ½" more, increasing 1 stitch at end of

last (WS) row—34 stitches. Cut A. **Begin Chart Pattern: Row 1** (RS) Join 2 strands MC and work row 1 of Chart Pattern over 29 stitches, place remaining 5 stitches on hold (for buttonhole band). Complete to correspond to right front, reversing neck shaping by binding off at beginning of WS rows.

Sleeves

With 2 strands A, cast on 33 stitches. Work in k1, p1 rib for 1". Work in Chart Pattern, AT SAME TIME, increase 1 stitch each side (working increases into pattern) on 5th row, then every 6th row 7 times more—49 stitches. Work even until piece measures 11½" from beginning. Bind off.

Finishing

Block pieces. Sew shoulders.

Button band

Place 5 right front band stitches onto needle, ready to work a RS row. Work in k1, p1 rib until band, slightly stretched, measures same length as front to neck. Bind off. Sew band to front edge. Place 4 markers on band for buttons, with the first and last ½" from upper and lower edges, and 2 others spaced evenly between.

Buttonhole Band

Place 5 left front band stitches onto needle, ready to work a RS row. Join A and work as for button band, working buttonhole rows to correspond to 3 top button markers.

INTERMEDIATE

LOOSE FIT

2–4 years

A 29¾"
B 12½"
C 18½"

10cm/4"

20

16

• over stockinette stitch (knit on RS, purl on WS) with yarn doubled

1 2 **3** 4 5 6

• Light weight
MC • 650 yds
A • 100 yds
B • 50 yds
C • 120 yds

• 5mm/US 8, or size to obtain gauge

• four 19mm/¾"

• stitch holders
• stitch markers

Page 27 BERROCO Mohair Light (mohair, polyester; 40g; 185yds) in Red (MC), Plum (A), Yellow (B), and Green (C)

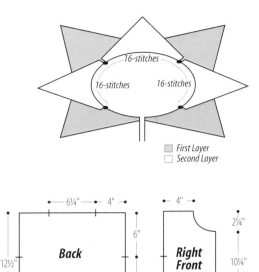

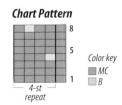

Collar

With RS facing and 2 strands C, pick up and knit 64 stitches evenly around neck edge (excluding bands).

Next row Purl.

Work four 16-stitch leaves: * **Next row** (RS) K16, turn work.

Next row (WS) K16, turn work. Repeat from * once more.

Decrease row (RS) K2tog, knit to last 2 stitches of leaf, k2tog.

Next row (WS) Knit. Repeat decrease row every RS row 6 times more—2 stitches.

Next row (WS) Knit 2.

Next row (RS) K2tog. Fasten off. One leaf complete. [Join yarn to next 16 stitches and work leaf] 3 times.

Work three 16-stitch leaves: With RS facing and 2 strands C, pick up and knit 16 stitches between center of first leaf and center of 2nd leaf. Work leaf as before. Work 2 more leaves between centers of next 2 leaves from first layer.

Place markers on front and back 6" down from shoulders for armholes. Sew top of sleeves between markers. Sew side and sleeve seams. Sew on buttons.

Chart Pattern

Color key
MC
B

4-st repeat

6

Heart
Pockets

6

Designed by Vicki Square

Heart Pockets

it's
easy
...go
for it!

EASY+

B   A

LOOSE FIT

12 months (2, 4) years
A 24 (26, 27¾)"
B 10 (11, 11½)"

10cm/4"

28 ▦ 21

• over stockinette stitch
(knit on RS, purl on WS)

1 2 3 **4** 5 6

• Medium weight
MC • 200 (300, 400) yds
A, C • 50 yds each
B, D, E, F • small amount of each

• 4mm/US 6,
or size to obtain gauge

&

• stitch markers & holders

• size 4mm/G

• three 19mm/¾"

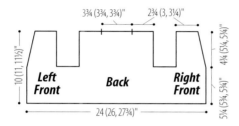

10 (11, 11½)"

3¾ (3¾, 3¾)"   2¾ (3, 3¼)"

Left Front   **Back**   **Right Front**

4¾ (5¼, 5¾)"

5¾ (5¾, 5¾)"

24 (26, 27¾)"

Notes

1 See *Techniques*, page 110, for 3-needle bind-off, SSK, single crochet (sc), slip stitch, and intarsia knitting. **2** Body is worked in one piece to underarm, then divided, and fronts and back are worked separately. **3** When working heart motif on pocket, use 3 separate lengths of yarn (1 each side for A, 1 in center with C). At color changes, bring new color under old to twist yarns and prevent holes.

Body

With MC, cast on 126 (136, 146) stitches. Begin with a knit row, work in stockinette stitch as follows: 10 (12, 12) rows MC, 2 rows each of A, B, C, D, E and F. Continue with MC until piece measures 5¼ (5¾, 5¾)" from beginning, end with a WS row.

Divide for fronts and back

Next row (RS) K26 (28, 30) (right front), bind off 13 (15, 16) stitches (underarm), knit until there are 48 (50, 54) stitches on right needle (for back), bind off 13 (15, 16) stitches (underarm), knit to end (left front).
Next row (WS) P26 (28, 30) stitches of left front and place all other stitches on hold.

Left Front

Shape V-neck

Decrease row (RS) Knit to last 3 stitches (neck edge), k2tog, k1. Repeat Decrease row every other row 8 (9, 7) times more, then every 4th row 3 (3, 5) times—14 (15, 17) stitches. Work even until armhole measures 4¾ (5¼, 5¾)". Place stitches on hold.

Right Front

With WS facing, join yarn and work to correspond to left front, reversing neck shaping by working k1, SSK at beginning of RS rows.

Back

With WS facing, join yarn and work even until armhole measures same length as fronts, end with a RS row.

Size 2 CLASSIC ELITE Provence (cotton; 100g; 256yds) in Blue (MC), Green (A), Purple (B), Fuchsia (C), Red (D), Orange (E), and Yellow (F)

Join shoulders

Fold left front so that stitches are parallel with back, with RS together. Join 14 (15, 17) left front shoulder stitches to same number of back stitches, using 3-needle bind-off, then bind off 20 stitches of back neck, slip stitch remaining on right needle to left needle and bind off stitches of right front shoulder together with remaining 14 (15, 17) stitches of back.

Finishing

Block piece.

Edgings

Note Work approximately 2 sc for every 3 rows of knitting, and 1 sc for each knit stitch.

Place 3 markers along right front edge for button loops, the first ½" below beginning of neck shaping, the last ½" above lower edge, and 1 more spaced evenly between. With RS facing, crochet hook and C, begin at "side seam" and work 1 row sc around entire edge of vest, working 2 sc at beginning of right and left front V-neck shaping, and 3 sc at each lower front corner. Work another row sc, working button loops (by chain 3, skip 2 sc) along right front edge at markers. End with slip stitch in first sc. Fasten off. With C, work 1 row sc around each armhole.

Pocket

With A, cast on 19 stitches. Work 16 rows of Heart Chart. Bind off. Using photo as guide, center pocket over stripes on right front and sew in place. Sew on buttons.

Heart Chart

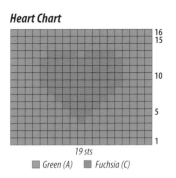

19 sts

■ Green (A)   ■ Fuchsia (C)

7 Sunny Days

Designed by Stephanie Gildersleeve

INTERMEDIATE

B | A | C

LOOSE FIT

12 (18, 24) months
A 25½ (27, 28¾)"
B 12½ (14, 15)"
C 12½ (14, 18)"

10cm/4"

22 / 19

over stockinette stitch
(knit on RS, purl on WS)

1 2 3 **4** 5 6
• Medium weight
MC • 360 (450, 550) yds
A & B • 185 yds each
C • 50 yds

• 3.75mm/US 5, or size to obtain gauge

• five 19mm/¾"

• stitch markers

Notes

1 See *Techniques*, page 110, for intarsia and duplicate stitch. **2** Use a separate strand of yarn for each color section of sunflower motif. Do not carry unused colors behind work for more than 2 stitches. **3** Work orange details in duplicate stitch after pieces are knitted.

Back

With MC, cast on 59 (63, 67) stitches. Work in k1, p1 rib for 1½ (1½, 2)", increasing 1 stitch on last (WS) row—60 (64, 68) stitches.
Beginning and ending as indicated for back, work rows 7-36 (3-36, 1-36) of Sunflower Chart. Piece measures approximately 7 (7¾, 8½)" from beginning.
Shape armholes
Bind off 4 stitches at beginning of next 2 rows—52 (56, 60) stitches. Work even through chart row 64 (68, 70). Armhole measures approximately 5 (5¾, 6)".
Shape neck
Next row (RS) K16 (16, 18), join new yarn, bind off center 20 (24, 24) stitches, work to end. Working both sides at same time, purl 1 row. Bind off.

Left Front

With MC, cast on 28 (30, 32) stitches. Work rib as for back. Work Sunflower Chart, beginning and ending as indicated for left front, until piece measures same length as back to underarm.
Next row (RS) Bind off 4 stitches, work to end—24 (26, 28) stitches. Work even through chart row 61 (63, 65). Armhole measures approximately 4½ (4¾, 5)".
Shape neck
Next row (WS) Bind off 4 stitches, work to end. Decrease 1 stitch at neck edge every row 4 (6, 6) times—16 (16, 18) stitches. Bind off.

Right Front

Work as for left front, reversing armhole and neck shaping. Begin and end chart as indicated for right front.

Sleeves

With MC, cast on 29 (31, 35) stitches. Work in k1, p1 rib for 2", increasing 1 stitch on last (WS) row—30 (32, 36) stitches. Continue in stockinette stitch, increasing 1 stitch each side on 3rd row, then every other row 8 (11, 0) times more, every 4th row 2 (2, 12) times—52

Page 31 Size 12 months REYNOLDS Saucy (cotton; 100g; 185 yds) in Pink (MC), Yellow (A), Brown (B), and Orange (C)

Sunflower Chart

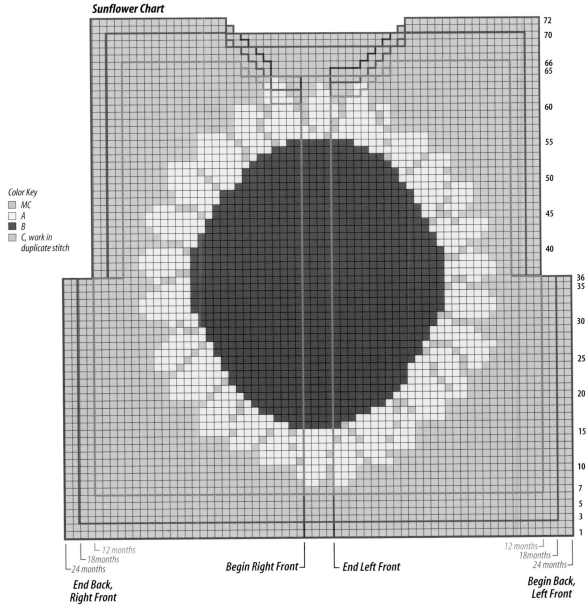

Color Key
- MC
- A
- B
- C, work in duplicate stitch

72
70
66
65
60
55
50
45
40
36
35
30
25
20
15
10
7
5
3
1

12 months
18months
24 months

End Back,
Right Front

Begin Right Front

End Left Front

12 months
18months
24 months

Begin Back,
Left Front

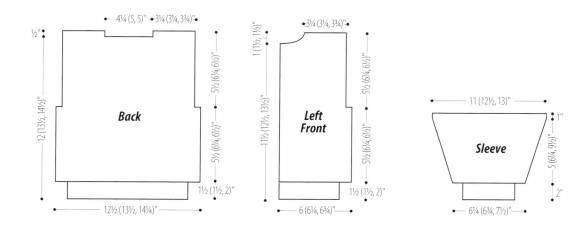

Back

4¼ (5, 5)" • 3¼ (3¼, 3¾)"

½"

12 (13½, 14½)"

5½ (6¼, 6½)"

5½ (6¼, 6½)"

1½ (1½, 2)"

12½ (13½, 14¼)"

Left Front

3¼ (3¼, 3¾)"

1 (1½, 1½)"

11½ (12½, 13½)"

5½ (6¼, 6½)"

5½ (6¼, 6½)"

1½ (1½, 2)"

6 (6¼, 6¾)"

Sleeve

11 (12½, 13)"

1"

5 (6¼, 9½)"

2"

6¼ (6¾, 7½)"

(60, 62) stitches. Piece measures approximately 7 (8¼, 11½)" from beginning. Work even for 1". Bind off.

Finishing

Block pieces. Sew top of sleeves to straight edges of armholes. Sew straight portion at top of sleeves to bound-off armhole stitches. Sew side and sleeve seams.

Button band

With RS facing and MC, pick up and knit 4 stitches for every 5 rows along right front edge. Work in k1, p1 rib for 1". Bind off in rib. Place 5 markers for buttons along band, with the

first ½" from top edge, the last ½" from lower edge and 3 others spaced evenly between.

Buttonhole band

Work as for button band, working buttonholes (work k2tog, yo) to correspond to each button marker when band measures ½".

Neck band

With RS facing and MC, pick up and knit stitches evenly spaced along neck edge. Work in k1, p1 rib for 2 rows. Bind off in rib. Work orange flower details in duplicate stitch as shown on chart. Sew on buttons.

4-Tam
Pram Set

8

These eye-catching, structurally unusual garments are fun to knit and the concise instructions are easily memorized. Be prepared to do some explaining if someone asks what you are knitting, as the piece will not look anything like the finished garment until removed from the needles and folded.

Designed by Debbie New

4-Tam Pram Set

Notes

1 See *Techniques*, page 110, pick up and knit, left-slanting Make 1 (M1L), SSK, stockinette stitch grafting, and twisted cord. **2** Sweater is made of 2 hexagon shapes; pants and hat are made of 1 octagon shape each. Fold and join pieces as shown in diagrams. **3** Change to circular needle (from dpns) when necessary. **4** Use slip knot circular cast-on for all pieces.

HAT

With dpn and MC, cast on 4 stitches divided evenly over 4 dpn. Join and work in rounds as follows:

Round 1 [Yo, k1] 4 times—8 stitches.
Round 2 [K1 through back loop, place marker (pm), k1] 4 times, using a different color for last marker.
Round 3 [M1L, k1, byo, slip marker (sm), k1] 4 times—16 stitches.
Round 4 Knit.

Round 5 [M1L, k1, byo, pm, k1, M1L, k1, byo, sm, k1] 4 times—32 stitches (4 stitches between markers).
Rounds 6 and 7 With CC, knit.
Rounds 8, 10, 11 With MC, knit.
Rounds 9 and 12 With MC, [M1L, knit to marker, byo, sm, k1] 8 times.
Repeat Rounds 6-12 until there are 18 (20) stitches between markers, ending with Round 9 (12). With MC (CC), knit 1 round, purl 1 round.
Shape crown
Size 3 months only :
Rounds 1, 5, 7, and 8 With MC, knit.
Rounds 2 and 6 With MC, [k2tog, knit to 2 stitches before marker, SSK, sm, k1] 8 times.
Rounds 3 and 4 With CC, knit.
Round 9 Repeat Round 2—12 stitches between markers.
Rounds 10 and 11 With CC, knit.
Round 12 With MC, knit.

All • 3.75mm/US 5 or size to obtain gauge, 40cm/16" and 60cm/24" long
• 2.75mm/US 2, 60cm/24" long

All • five 3.75mm/US 5

Sweater • seven 13mm/½"

&

All • stitch markers and holders

Page 35 Size 6 months ROWAN Wool Cotton (wool, cotton; 50g; 123 yds) in Blue, Dark Green, and Light Green

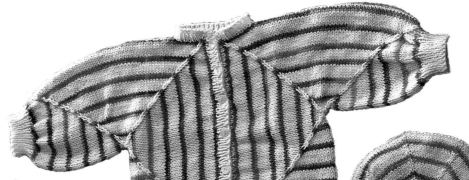

Size 6 months only:

Rounds 1, 3, and 4 With MC, knit.

Rounds 2 and 5 With MC, [k2tog, knit to 2 stitches before marker, SSK, sm, k1] 8 times.

Rounds 6 and 7 With CC, knit.

Round 8 With MC, knit.

Round 9 Repeat Round 2—14 stitches between markers.

Rounds 10 and 11 With MC, knit.

Band

Change to smaller circular needle. Work ¾" in k1, p1 rib. Bind off in rib pattern.

BACKWARD YARN OVER (BYO)

1 Bring yarn from back to front over needle, then to back again under needle. Knit next stitch on left needle.

2 On following round, knit into the front loop of the yarn over to twist it.

3 The result is a right-slanting increase.

SLIP KNOT CIRCULAR CAST-ON

1 Make a slip knot loop with the cut tail rather than the ball end.

2 Work into loop as follows: * yo, k1; repeat from * until desired number of stitches has been cast on.

3 Arrange stitches on 3 or 4 double-pointed needles, pull tail slightly, then begin knitting around, working into the back loops of yarn-overs on the first round. Work several more rounds, then pull tail to close center.

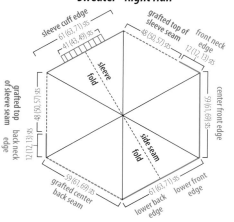

Sweater - Right Half

sleeve cuff edge
61 (63, 71) sts
41 (43, 49) sts
grafted top of sleeve seam
48 (50, 57) sts
front neck edge
12 (12, 13) sts
sleeve fold
grafted top of sleeve seam
48 (50, 57) sts
center front edge
59 (61, 69) sts
side seam fold
back neck edge
12 (12, 13) sts
grafted center back seam
59 (61, 69) sts
lower back edge
lower back edge
61 (63, 71) sts
lower front edge

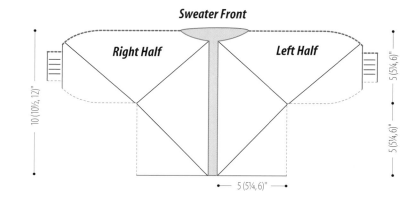

Sweater Front

Right Half   Left Half

10 (10½, 12)"
5 (5¼, 6)"
5 (5¼, 6)"
5 (5¼, 6)"

SWEATER
Right Half
With dpns and MC, cast on 6 stitches, using slipknot circular cast-on. Divide stitches evenly over 3 dpns. Join and work in rounds as follows:

Round 1 [Yo, k1] 6 times—12 stitches.

Round 2 [K1 through back loop, place marker (pm), k1] 6 times, using a different color for last marker.

Round 3 [M1L, k1, byo, slip marker (sm), k1] 6 times—24 stitches.

Round 4 Knit.

Round 5 [M1L, k3, byo, sm, k1] 6 times—36 stitches.

Rounds 6 and 7 With CC, [M1L, knit to marker, byo, sm, k1] 6 times—60 stitches.

Rounds 8 and 12 With MC, knit.

Rounds 9, 10 and 11 With MC, repeat Round 6—96 stitches (16 stitches between markers).

[Repeat Rounds 6-12] 4 (4, 5) times more, then work Rounds 6-7 (6-9, 6-7) once—60 (62, 70) stitches between markers.

Sleeve cuff
With smaller circular needle and MC, work back and forth in rows as follows:

Row 1 (RS) K0 (1, 2), [k2tog, k1] 19 (20, 22) times, [k2tog] 1 (0, 0) time, k0 (0, 1), remove marker (rm), k1, turn.

Row 2 P1, [k1, p1] 20 (21, 24) times, rm, turn—41 (43, 49) cuff stitches.

Row 3 K1, [p1, k1] 20 (21, 24) times. Continue in k1, p1 rib until cuff measures 1". Bind off in rib pattern. Cut yarn, leaving a long tail for seaming. Fold hexagon at fold line indicated on diagram and, using tail, sew side of cuff rib, then graft 48 (50, 57) stitches of top of sleeve together.

Place stitches of each section onto separate holders as follows (removing markers): 12 (12, 13) back neck stitches, 59 (61, 69) stitches for center back seam, 61 (63, 71) stitches for lower edge of back and front, 59 (61, 69) stitches for center front edge, and 12 (12, 13) front neck stitches.

Left Half
Work as for right half, ending with grafting top of sleeve.

Place stitches of each section onto separate holders

Page 37 Size 3 months PATON'S Look at Me (acrylic, nylon; 50g; 152 yds) in White (MC) and Variegated (CC)

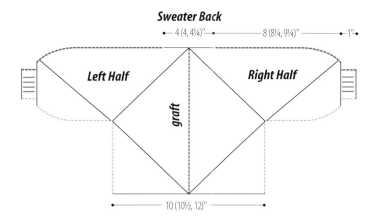

Sweater Back

4 (4, 4¼)" — 8 (8¼, 9¼)" — 1"

Left Half · Right Half

graft

10 (10½, 12)"

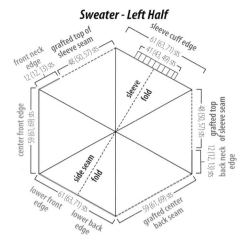

Sweater - Left Half

front neck edge · 12 (12, 13) sts
grafted top of sleeve seam · 48 (50, 57) sts
sleeve cuff edge · 61 (63, 71) sts
41 (43, 49) sts
center front edge · 59 (61, 69) sts
sleeve fold
grafted top of sleeve seam · 48 (50, 57) sts
back neck of sleeve seam edge · 12 (12, 13) sts
side seam fold
lower front edge · 61 (63, 71) sts
lower back edge
grafted center back seam · 59 (61, 69) sts

as follows: 12 (12, 13) stitches for front neck, 59 (61, 69) stitches for center front edge, 61 (63, 71) stitches for lower edge of front and back, 59 (61, 69) stitches for center back seam, and 12 (12, 13) stitches for back neck.

Finishing

Orient both halves with 59 (61, 69) center back seam stitches facing each other. With MC, graft stitches together.

Front, neck and lower border

With RS facing, begin at center back seam and slip stitches from holders on right half onto smaller circular needle as follows: 61 (63, 71) stitches of lower edge, 59 (61, 69) stitches of center front edge, and 24 (24, 26) stitches of neck edge, then continue to slip stitches of left half, ending at center back seam—288 (296, 332) stitches. With MC, join and work in rounds as follows:

Round 1 *K2, [knit into front and back of next stitch (kf&b), k4] 11 (12, 13) times, [kf&b, k2] 1 (0, 1) time, pm*, repeat from* to* once more, k2, [kf&b, k4] 4 times, kf&b, k1 (1, 3), pick up and knit 1 stitch from end of grafted row, k0 (0, 2), [kf&b, k4] 4 times, kf&b, k2, pm, repeat from* to* twice (except do not pm after 2nd repeat), k1, pick up and knit 1 stitch from end of grafted row, pm for end of round—348 (356, 400) stitches.

Round 2 [K1, p1] 36 (37, 42) times, byo, sm, k1, M1L, *p1, [k1, p1] 35 (36, 41) times, byo, sm, k1, M1L*, p1, [k1, p1] 28 (28, 30) times, byo, sm, k1, M1L, repeat from* to* once, p1, *k1, p1; repeat from* to end—356 (364, 408) stitches.

Round 3 [Rib to marker, byo, sm, k1, M1L] 4 times, rib to end—364 (372, 416) stitches.

Round 4 Rib to marker, byo, sm, k1, M1L, [p1, k1] 0 (1, 0) time, [yo, k2tog, (p1, k1) 5 (5, 6) times] 6 times, yo, k2tog, p1, [byo, sm, k1, M1L, rib to marker] 3 times—372 (380, 424) stitches.

Round 5 Repeat Round 3—380 (388, 432) stitches. Bind off in rib.

Tighten cast-on loops and secure. Sew on buttons. Block piece.

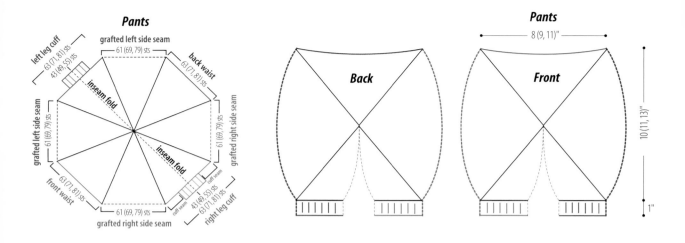

PANTS

Work as for right half of sweater with these changes: Cast on 8 stitches, divided evenly over 4 dpn; work repeats 8 times, instead of 6. At end of Round 7, there are 80 stitches (10 stitches between markers). [Repeat Rounds 6–12] 4 (5, 6) times more, then work Rounds 6–9 (6–7, 6–7) once—62 (70, 80) stitches between markers.

Leg cuffs

With smaller circular needle and MC, work back and forth in rows over left cuff edge as follows:

Row 1 K0 (1, 0), [k1, k2tog] 20 (22, 26) times, k1 (2, 1), remove marker (rm), k1, turn.

Row 2 P1, [k1, p1] 21 (24, 27) times, rm, turn—43 (49, 55) stitches.

Row 3 K1, [p1, k1] 21 (24, 27) times. Continue in k1, p1 rib until cuff measures 1". Bind off in rib pattern. Cut yarn, leaving a long tail. Fold octagon at fold line indicated on diagram and, using tail, sew side of cuff rib, then graft 61 (69, 79) left side seam stitches together. Skip 63 (71, 81) front waist stitches, and next 61 (69, 79) right side seam stitches, and work cuff over next 63 (71, 81) right leg cuff stitches as for left leg. Complete as for left leg, grafting side seam stitches together.

Waistband

With smaller circular needle and MC, work k1, p1 rib in rounds over remaining 126 (142, 162) front and back waist stitches for ¾".

Next round *Yo, k2tog; repeat from*. Rib 2 rounds more. Bind off in rib pattern.

Finishing

Close center hole and block piece. With MC, make a 28" twisted cord. Thread through eyelets and tie in front.

Fair Isle
Fun

9

Even with added color patterning, small projects are easy to knit. In a kid-friendly cotton yarn and sophisticated colors, your little one will enjoy wearing the sweater and hat as much as you'll enjoy making it!

Designed by Mags Kandis

Fair Isle Fun

INTERMEDIATE

LOOSE FIT

PULLOVER
6 (12, 24) months
A 20½ (24, 26)"
B 10 (11, 12)"
C 12 (13½, 14½)"

HAT
Circumference 17¼"
Length 6¼"

10cm/4"

24

18

• over chart pattern, using larger needles

1 2 3 **4** 5 6

• Medium weight
For both hat and pullover
A • 110 (140, 160) yds
B–F • 60 (75, 85) yds each

• 3.75mm/US 5 and 4.5mm/US 7, or size to obtain gauge

• three 13mm/½"

&

• stitch markers

42

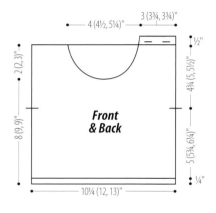

Front & Back

— 4 (4½, 5¼)" — 3 (3¾, 3¾)"
½"
2 (2,3)"
8 (9, 9)"
4¾ (5, 5½)"
5 (5¾, 6¼)"
¼"
— 10¼ (12, 13)" —

Sleeve

— 9½ (10, 11)" —
6¾ (7¼, 7¾)"
¼"
— 5¾ (5¾, 6¾)" —

Note

See *Techniques*, page 110, for twisted cord.

PULLOVER
Back

With smaller needles and A, cast on 42 (50, 54) stitches. Purl 1 row. Knit 1 row. Purl 2 rows, increasing 4 stitches evenly across on 2nd row—46 (54, 58) stitches. Change to larger needles. Beginning and ending as indicated, work Chart A through row 58 (64, 70). Piece measures approximately 10 (11, 12)" from beginning.

Button band

Next row (RS) With A, bind off 32 (37, 41) stitches, knit to end—14 (17, 17) stitches. Purl 1 row. Bind off all stitches purlwise.

Front

Work as for back through chart row 46 (52, 52). Piece measures approximately 8 (9, 9)" from beginning.

Shape neck

Next row (RS) Work 19 (23, 24) stitches in pattern, join a 2nd ball of yarn and bind off center 8 (8, 10) stitches, work in pattern to end. Working both sides at same time, decrease 1 stitch at each neck edge every row

Page 41 Size 24 months MISSION FALLS TRADING Softball Cotton (cotton; 50g; 84yds) in Black (A), Gold (B), Purple (C), Coral (D), Green (E), and Blue (F)

5 (6, 7) times—14 (17, 17) stitches each side. Work even through chart row 58 (64, 70).

Buttonhole band

Work stitches of left shoulder only as follows: With A, knit 1 row, purl 1 row.

Buttonhole row (RS) *K2 (3, 3), k2tog, yo twice, k2tog; repeat from* once more, k2 (3, 3).

Next row (WS) Purl, working into front of first yo and into back of 2nd yo. Bind off purlwise. Bind off stitches of right shoulder.

Sleeves

With smaller needles and A, cast on 24 (24, 28) stitches. Purl 1 row. Knit 1 row. Purl 2 rows, increasing 2 stitches evenly across on 2nd row—26 (26, 30) stitches. Change to larger needles. Beginning and ending as indicated, work Chart B, AT SAME TIME, increase 1 stitch each side (working increases into pattern) on 5th row, then every 4th row 7 (8, 9) times more—42 (44, 50) stitches. Work even through chart row 40 (44, 46). Piece measures approximately 7 (7½, 8)" from beginning. Bind off all stitches.

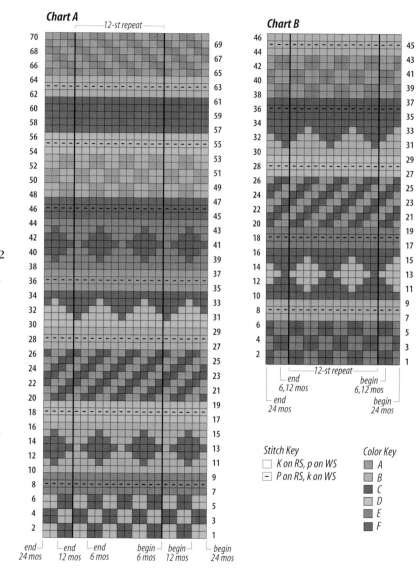

Chart A

Chart B

Stitch Key
☐ K on RS, p on WS
⊟ P on RS, k on WS

Color Key
A
B
C
D
E
F

Chart C

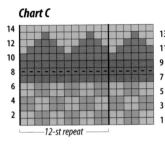

Stitch Key
☐ K on RS, p on WS
⊟ P on RS, k on WS

Color Key
■ A
☐ B
■ C
☐ D
☐ E
■ F

Finishing

Block pieces. Sew right shoulder.

Neckband

With RS facing, smaller needles and A, begin at top of buttonhole band and pick up and knit 50 (52, 64) stitches evenly around neck edge.

Row 1 (WS) Knit.

Row 2 (buttonhole row) P2tog, yo twice, p2tog, purl to end.

Row 3 Knit, working into front of first yo and into back of 2nd yo.

Row 4 Purl.

Bind off loosely knitwise. Lap buttonhole band over buttonband and tack in place at armhole edge. Place markers 4¾ (5, 5½)" down from shoulders on front and back for armholes. Sew sleeves between markers. Sew side and sleeve seams. Sew on buttons opposite buttonholes.

HAT

With smaller needles and A, cast on 78 stitches.

Purl 1 row. Knit 1 row. Purl 2 rows. Change to larger needles.

Work 14 rows of Chart C. With A, knit 2 rows, purl 1 row.

Next row (WS) Purl, decreasing 1 stitch at center—77 stitches.

Shape crown

Row 1 (RS) With A, *k9, k2tog; repeat from* to end—70 stitches.

Row 2 and all WS rows Purl with color of preceding row.

Row 3 *K8, k2tog; repeat from* to end—63 stitches.

Row 5 With D, *k7, k2tog; repeat from* to end—56 stitches.

Row 7 *K6, k2tog; repeat from* to end—49 stitches.

Row 9 With A, *k5, k2tog; repeat from* to end—42 stitches.

Row 11 *K4, k2tog; repeat from* to end—35 stitches.

Row 13 With E, *k3, k2tog; repeat from* to end—28 stitches.

Row 15 *K2, k2tog; repeat from* to end—21 stitches.

Row 17 With A, *k1, k2tog; repeat from* to end—14 stitches.

Row 18 Purl.

Fasten off and pass yarn through remaining stitches, tighten and secure.

Finishing

Sew back seam. Make two 15" twisted cords using 1 strand each of C and D. Attach to each side of hat on WS.

Zoe's First
Christmas

10

This cardigan for little girls is holiday-hued, yet packed with enough detail for truly timeless appeal. Machine-washable wool keeps mother, baby, and knitter happy. And when Zoe has finally outgrown this sweater, it will be ready to be handed down again and again.

Designed by Nancy Bush

Zoe's First Christmas

INTERMEDIATE

LOOSE FIT

12–18 months (2–4 years)
A 23 (30½)"
B 12½ (16)"
C 12½ (18½)"

10cm/4"

28

26

• over stockinette stitch (knit on RS, purl on WS), using larger needle

1 2 **3** 4 5 6

• Light weight
MC • 465 (580) yds
A and B • 116 (116) yds each

• 2.75mm/US 2 and 3.5mm/US 4, or size to obtain gauge, 60cm/24" long

• five 13mm/½"

&

• stitch markers and holders

Notes

1 See *Techniques*, page 110, for S2KP2, 3-needle bind-off, long-tail cast-on, and loop cast-on. **2** Body of sweater is worked in one piece to underarm, then divided and fronts and backs are worked separately.

Body

With larger needle and 1 strand each MC and A held together, make a slipknot and place it on needle (this stitch will be removed later and is not counted in the total stitch count). With A over your index finger and MC over your thumb, cast on 147 (195) stitches, using long-tail cast-on.

Work Half Braid Edge

Row 1 (WS) *P1 MC, p1 A; repeat from*, end p1 MC, remove slipknot from needle.

Row 2 Bring both yarns to front, p1 MC, *bring A yarn over MC and p1 A, bring MC yarn over A and p1 MC; repeat from* to end. Break off A.

Next row (WS) P37 (49), place marker (pm), p73 (97), pm, purl to end.

Begin Chart A: Row 1 (RS) Work

12-stitch repeat of chart 3 (4) times, work last stitch of chart, slip marker (sm), work 12-stitch repeat of chart 6 (8) times, work last stitch of chart, sm, work 12-stitch repeat of chart 3 (4) times, work last stitch of chart. Continue in pattern as established until piece measures 7½ (9½)" from beginning, end with a WS row.

Divide for armholes

Next row (RS) K37 (49) stitches of right front and place these stitches on hold, removing marker, k73 (97) stitches of back and place these stitches on hold, removing marker, knit to end.

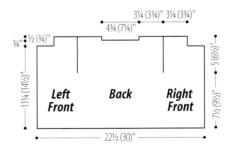

3¼ (3¾)" 3¼ (3¾)"
4¾ (7¼)"
¾" ½ (¾)"
11¼ (14½)"
5 (6½)"
7½ (9½)"

Left Front **Back** **Right Front**

22½ (30)"

Page 45 Size 12–18 months DALE OF NORWAY Falk (machine-washable wool; 50g; 116 yards) in Red (MC), White (A), and Green (B)

Chart A

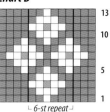

Chart B

Chart C

Chart D

2-st repeat

Color Key

⬛ MC
⬜ A
⬛ B

Stitch Key

⬜ Knit on RS, purl on WS
⊙ Yo
▲ S2KP2

Left Front

Next row (WS) Purl.

[Knit 1 row, purl 1 row] 0 (2) times.

Begin Chart B: Row 1 (RS) Work first 3 stitches of chart, then work 6-stitch repeat across to last 4 stitches, work last 4 stitches of chart. Continue in pattern as established through chart row 13. With MC, [purl 1 row, knit 1 row] 1 (2) times.

Begin Chart C: Row 1 (WS) Reading chart from left to right, work last 11 stitches of chart, then work 12-stitch repeat across to last 2 stitches, work first 2 stitches of chart. Continue in pattern as established through chart row 9. With MC, knit 1 row, [purl 1 row, knit 1 row] 0 (1) time. Armhole measures approximately 3¾ (5)".

Shape neck

Next row (WS) With MC, bind off 16 (24) stitches, purl to end—21 (25) stitches.

Begin Chart D: Row 1 (RS) Work 2-stitch repeat across to last stitch, work last stitch of chart. Continue in pattern as established through chart row 5. With MC, [purl 1 row, knit 1 row] 1 (2) times. Armhole measures approximately 5 (6½)". Place stitches on hold.

Right Front

With WS facing, join MC and work as for left front through row 9 of Chart C. With MC, [knit 1 row, purl 1 row] 1 (2) times.

Shape neck

Begin Chart D: Next row (RS) With MC, bind off 16 (24) stitches, then beginning with 2nd stitch of chart, work Chart D to end—21 (25) stitches. Continue in pattern as established through chart row 5. With MC, [purl 1 row, knit 1 row] 1 (2) times. Place stitches on hold.

Back

With WS facing, join MC and work as for fronts through row 9 of Chart C. With MC, [knit 1 row, purl 1 row] 1 (2) times.

Begin Chart D: Row 1 (RS) Work 2-stitch repeat across to last stitch, work last stitch of chart. Continue in pattern as established through chart row 4. Armhole measures approximately 4½ (5¾)".

Shape neck

Next row (RS) Work 21 (25) stitches in pattern, join 2nd ball of B and bind off center 31 (47) stitches, join 2nd ball of MC and work in pattern to end. Break B. Working both sides at same time

with MC, [purl 1 row, knit 1 row] 1 (2) times. Place stitches on hold.

Sleeves

With smaller needles and MC, cast on 30 (38) stitches. *With MC, knit 2 rows, with A, knit 2 rows; repeat from* twice more, with MC, knit 2 rows. Break A. Continue with MC only. Change to larger needles. **Next row** (RS) Knit, increasing 10 stitches evenly across—40 (48) stitches. Continue in stockinette stitch, increasing 1 stitch each side every other row 8 (4) times, then every 4th row 5 (14) times—66 (84) stitches. Work even until piece measures 7¼ (11¼)" from beginning. Bind off.

Finishing

Block pieces. Join shoulders, using 3-needle bind-off. Sew sleeves into armholes. Sew sleeve seams.
Button band
With RS facing, smaller needle and MC, pick up and knit 2 out of 3 stitches along left front edge. Knit 2 rows. Bind off knitwise.
Buttonhole band
Place 5 markers along right front edge for buttonholes, with the first 1" above lower edge, the last ½" below neck edge, and 3 others spaced evenly between. Work as for buttonband, working buttonholes on 2nd knit row at markers as follows: slip 1 stitch purlwise with yarn in back (wyib), [slip 1 stitch purlwise wyib, pass 2nd stitch on right needle over first stitch] twice, slip stitch from right needle to left needle, loop cast on 2 stitches onto right needle.
Neckband
With RS facing, smaller needle and MC, pick up and knit 5 out of 6 stitches along right front neck edge to shoulder, 2 stitches along side of back neck, 1 stitch for every bound-off stitch of back neck, 2 stitches along side of neck, and 5 out of 6 stitches along left front neck edge. Knit 2 rows. Bind off knitwise. Sew on buttons.

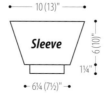

10 (13)"

Sleeve

6 (10)"

1¼"

6¼ (7½)"

Here's slip stitch done in fun, kid-friendly colors. Three solids are used for striping and are set off by one matching variegated yarn. The slip-stitch pattern lets you do color the easy way, one color per row. Both the sweater and hat are made in an easy-care acrylic/nylon yarn that will stand up to playtime wear.

Designed by Katharine Hunt

Color At Play

INTERMEDIATE

LOOSE FIT

2 (4)
Pullover
A 26 (28)"
B 13½ (14¼)"
C 15 (17)"

Hat
Circumference 19 (20¼)"

10cm/4"

44
26
• over Chart B, using larger needle

1 2 **3** 4 5 6

• Light weight
Pullover and Hat
A • 400 (500) yds
B • 400 (500) yds
C • 65 (75) yds
D • 130 (150) yds

• 3.25mm/US 3 and 3.75mm/US 5,
or size to obtain gauge

• six 13mm/½"

• stitch holders

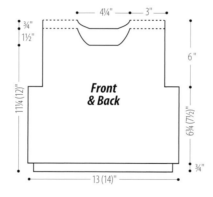

Front & Back

¾"
1½"
4¼" — 3"
11¼ (12)"
6 "
6¾ (7½)"
¾"
13 (14)"

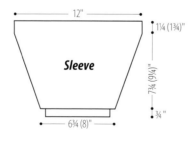

Sleeve

12"
1¼ (1¾)"
7¾ (9¼)"
¾ "
6¾ (8)"

Notes

1 See *Techniques*, page 110 for Make 1 knit (M1K) and purl (M1P), cable cast-on, twisted cord, and tassels. **2** Carry yarns loosely along side of work until needed.

Seed stitch

Row 1 * K1, p1; repeat from*.
Row 2 Knit the purl stitches and purl the knit stitches. Repeat Row 2 for seed stitch.

PULLOVER
Back

With smaller needles and A, cast on 70 (76) stitches. Work in seed stitch for 8 rows, increasing 14 (16) stitches evenly across last row—84 (92) stitches. Change to larger needles. Work 26 rows of Chart A twice. Cut C and D. Work rows 1-16 of Chart B once, then work rows 1-8 of chart 0 (1) time more. Piece measures approximately 7½ (8¼)" from beginning.
Shape armholes
Next 2 rows With A, bind off 8 (12) stitches, knit to end—68 stitches. Beginning with chart row 3, work Chart B until armhole measures approximately 5¼", end with chart row 10.
Shape neck
Next row (RS) Work 25 stitches, join 2nd ball

Page 49 Size 2 PATONS Look at Me! (acrylic, nylon; 50g; 152yds) in Variegated (A), Turquoise (B), Orange (C), and Yellow (D)

A
B
C
D

Chart A

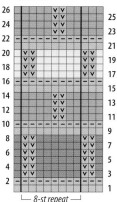

└─ 8-st repeat ─┘

Chart B

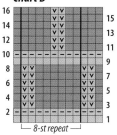

└─ 8-st repeat ─┘

Stitch Key

☐ Knit on RS

– Knit on WS

V Sl 1 purlwise with
yarn at WS of work

of yarn and bind off 18 stitches, work in pattern to end. Decrease 1 stitch at each neck edge every row 5 times—20 stitches each side. Work 2 rows even. Armhole measures approximately 6". Place stitches on hold.

Front

Work as for back until armhole measures approximately 3¾", end with chart row 10.

Shape neck

Next row (RS) Work 26 stitches, join 2nd ball of yarn and bind off 16 stitches, work in pattern to end. Decrease 1 stitch at each neck edge every row 6 times—20 stitches each side. Work 9 rows even. Armhole measures approximately 5¼". Place stitches on hold.

Sleeves

With smaller needles and A, cast on 36 (44) stitches. Work in seed stitch for 8 rows, increasing 8 stitches evenly across last row—44 (52) stitches. Change to larger needles. Work Chart B, AT SAME TIME, increase 1 stitch each side (working increases into pattern)

on 5th (7th) row, then every 4th (8th) row 8 (12) times, then every 6th row 8 (0) times—78 stitches. Piece measures approximately 8½ (10)" from beginning. Work even for approximately 1¼ (1¾)", ending with chart row 1 (9). Bind off knitwise with A.

Finishing

Block pieces.

Back neckband

With RS facing, smaller needles and A, pick up and knit 30 stitches along back neck edge. Knit 1 row.

Begin seed stitch: Row 1 (RS) *K1, p1; repeat from * to end.

Row 2 *P1, k1; repeat from * to end. Continue in seed stitch as follows:

Next row (RS) [K1, p1] 3 times, k2tog, p2tog, [k1, p1] 5 times, k2tog, p2tog, [k1, p1] 3 times—26 stitches. Work 2 rows even. Bind off in pattern.

Left back shoulder band

With WS facing, smaller needles and A, begin at armhole edge and knit 20 stitches from holder, then pick up and purl 4 stitches along edge of

neckband—24 stitches.
Next row (RS) P6, p2tog, p8, p2tog, p6—22 stitches. Work in seed stitch for 6 rows. Bind off in pattern.

Right back shoulder band

With WS facing, smaller needles and A, begin at neck edge and pick up and purl 4 stitches along edge of neckband, then knit 20 stitches from holder—24 stitches. Work as for left back shoulder band.

Front neckband

With RS facing, smaller needles and A, pick up and knit 42 stitches along front neck edge. Knit 1 row.
Begin seed stitch: Row 1 (RS) *K1, p1; repeat from * to end.
Row 2 *P1, k1; repeat from * to end. Continue in seed stitch as follows:
Next row (RS) [K1, p1] 5 times, k2tog, p2tog, [k1, p1] 7 times, k2tog, p2tog, [k1, p1] 5 times.
Work 1 row even.
Next row (RS) [K1, p1] 5 times, k2tog, p2tog, [k1, p1] 5 times, k2tog, p2tog, [k1, p1] 5 times—34 stitches. Bind off in pattern.

Right front shoulder band

Work as for left back shoulder band.

Left front shoulder band

Work as for right back shoulder band, working 3 buttonholes on 2nd seed stitch row as follows:
Note Slip stitches purlwise.
Next row (RS) Work 4 stitches, *with yarn in front (wyif) slip 1, [with yarn in back (wyib) slip 1, pass 2nd stitch on right needle over slip stitch] 3 times, slip last stitch on right needle back to left needle. Turn work. Move yarn to back and cable cast on 4 stitches onto left needle. Turn work. Wyib slip 1 from left needle, pass 2nd stitch on right needle over slip stitch, work 2 stitches; repeat from *twice more.
Place front shoulder bands on top of back shoulder bands and sew together at armhole edges. Sew right shoulder bands only together at neck edge. Sew 3 (functioning) buttons on left back shoulder band to correspond to buttonholes. Sew 3 (decorative) buttons on right shoulder band through both thicknesses. Sew top of sleeves to straight edges of armholes. Sew straight portion at top of sleeves to bound-off underarm stitches. Sew side and sleeve seams.

HAT

Notes 1 Use cable cast-on throughout.
2 For ease in working, mark RS of earflaps.

Earflaps (make 2)

With larger needles and A, cast on 7 (9) stitches. Work in seed stitch as follows:

Row 1 (RS) *K1, p1; repeat from*, end k1.
Rows 2, 4, and 6 P1, M1K, *p1, k1; repeat from* to last 2 stitches, p1, M1K, p1.
Rows 3 and 5 K1, M1P, *k1, p1; repeat from* to last 2 stitches, k1, M1P, k1.
Row 7 K1, *k1, p1; repeat from* to last 2 stitches, k2.
Row 8 P1, M1P, *k1, p1; repeat from* to last 2 stitches, k1, M1P, p1.
Rows 9 and 10 Repeat Rows 1 and 2.
Rows 11–14 Repeat Rows 7–10.
Rows 15 and 16 Repeat Rows 7 and 8—27 (29) stitches.
Row 17 Repeat Row 1.
Row 18 P1, *p1, k1; repeat from* to last 2 stitches, p2.

Repeat Rows 17 and 18 until flap measures 2 (3)" from beginning, end with a RS row. Cut yarn. Place stitches on hold.

Work band

With larger needles and A, cast on 13 (15) stitches (half of back), then with WS of one earflap facing, work in seed stitch across 27 (29) stitches from holder, cast on 37 (39) stitches (front), work in seed stitch across 27 (29) stitches of second ear flap, cast on 13 (15) stitches (remaining half of back)—117 (127) stitches.

Next row (RS) *P1, k1; repeat from* end p1. Work 5 (7) more rows in seed stitch, increasing 7 (5) stitches evenly across last row—124 (132) stitches.

Work 26 rows of Chart A.

Work rows 1–10 of Chart B, decreasing 3 (0) stitches evenly across last row—121 (132) stitches. Cut C and D.

Shape crown

Work rows 1–6 of Chart C. Change to smaller needles and continue through chart row 58—11 (12) stitches.

Next row (RS) With B, [k2tog] 5 (6) times, k1 (0). Break yarn, leaving a long tail. Draw yarn through remaining stitches, pull tightly to gather, and fasten securely to WS.

Finishing

Sew center back seam. With A, make 2 twisted cords (finished length approximately 6") and attach to end of each earflap, with the knotted end hanging down.

With A, make a 3" tassel and attach to top of hat.

Chart C

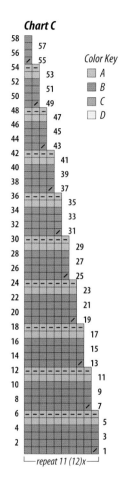

Color Key
- A
- B
- C
- D

Stitch Key
- ☐ Knit on RS
- ⊟ Knit on WS
- ☑ K2tog

12

Designed by Judith Goodman Johnson

Popovers

INTERMEDIATE

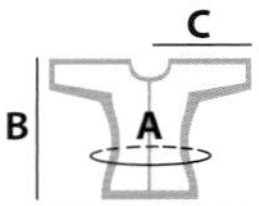
C
B
A
STANDARD FIT

6 (12, 24) months
A • 21 (23½, 25)"
B • 11 (12¼, 13½)"
C • 12 (12½, 15½)"

10cm/4"
28
22
• over Chart Pattern, using larger needles

1 2 **3** 4 5 6
• Light weight
MC • 420 (470, 560) yds
A and B • 130 yds each size

• 3.5mm/US 4 and 4mm/US 6, or size to obtain gauge, 40cm/16" long or longer

&
• stitch holders

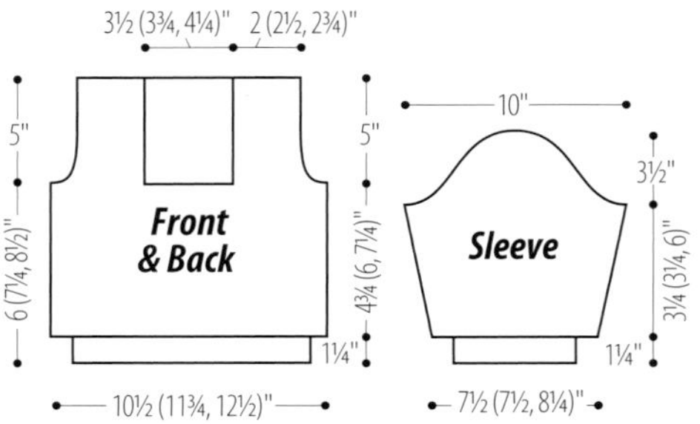
3½ (3¾, 4¼)"
2 (2½, 2¾)"
5"
5"
6 (7¼, 8½)"
Front & Back
4¾ (6, 7¼)"
1¼"
10½ (11¾, 12½)"
10"
3½"
Sleeve
3¼ (3¼, 6)"
1¼"
7½ (7½, 8¼)"

AMBER

Notes

1 See *Techniques*, page 110, for 3-needle bind-off and wrapping stitches on short rows. ***2*** Carry yarn along side of work until you need it again. To avoid long strands, catch the yarn once around the working yarn of another color. Since some colors are used over an odd number of rows, working with circular needles will minimize cutting and tying on new colors. If the color needed is waiting on the other edge of the piece, slide the knitting to the other end of the circular needle, and work from that side. This will mean occasionally working 2 consecutive RS or WS rows.

Back

With smaller needles and MC, cast on 52 (60, 64) stitches. Work in k1, p1 rib for 1¼", increasing 5 stitches evenly across last (WS) row—57 (65, 69) stitches. Change to larger needles. Beginning and ending as indicated for Back, work Chart Pattern until piece measures approximately 6 (7¼, 8½)" from beginning, end with chart row 10 (18, 2).

Shape armholes

Bind off 4 stitches at beginning of next 2 rows. Decease 1 stitch each side every RS row 4 times—41 (49, 53) stitches. Work even until armhole measures 5". Place stitches on hold.

Front

Work as for back until piece measures same length as back to underarm.

Shape armholes and neck

Next row (RS) Bind off 4 stitches, work until there are 15 (18, 19) stitches on right needle, join new yarn and bind off center 19 (21, 23) stitches, work to end. Working both sides at same time, work as follows: ***Next row*** (WS) Bind off 4 stitches, work to end of row. Continue to shape armhole each side as for back—11 (14, 15) stitches each side. Work even until piece measures same length as back to shoulder. Place stitches on hold.

Size 24 months SCHEWE, Escorial (superwash wool; 50g; 137 yds) in Light blue (MC) and Blue Heather (A) SCHEWE, Bistro (superwash wool, mercerized cotton; 50g; 122 yds) in Purple (B)

Sleeves

With smaller needles and MC, cast on 32 stitches. Work in k1, p1 rib for 1¼", increasing 9 (9, 13) stitches evenly across last (WS) row—41 (41, 45) stitches. Change to larger needles. Beginning and ending as indicated for sleeve, work chart row 13 (21, 9). Continue in pattern through chart row 24, then repeat rows 1–24, AT SAME TIME, increase 1 stitch each side (working increases into pattern) every 2nd (2nd, 6th) row 6 (6, 2) times, then every 4th (4th, 8th) row 1 (1, 3) times—55 stitches. Work even until piece measures approximately 4½ (4½, 7¼)" from beginning, end with chart row 10 (18, 2).

Shape cap

Bind off 4 stitches at beginning of next 2 rows,

Chart Pattern

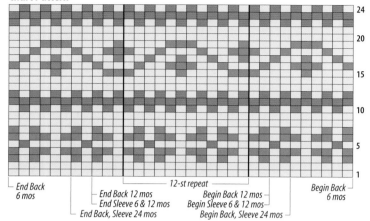

End Back 6 mos

End Back 12 mos
End Sleeve 6 & 12 mos
End Back, Sleeve 24 mos

12-st repeat

Begin Back 12 mos
Begin Sleeve 6 & 12 mos
Begin Back, Sleeve 24 mos

Begin Back 6 mos

Color Key
☐ MC   ▨ A   ▨ B

then 2 stitches at beginning of next 4 rows. Decrease 1 stitch each side every RS row 5 times. Work 1 row even. Bind off 2 stitches at beginning of next 8 rows. Bind off remaining 13 stitches.

Finishing

Block pieces. Join shoulders, using 3-needle bind-off as follows: Join 11 (14, 15) stitches of first shoulder, bind off back neck stitches until 11 (14, 15) stitches remain, join 2nd shoulder.

Collar

With RS facing, larger needles and MC, begin at lower corner of right neck and pick up and knit 36 stitches evenly along right front neck, 1 stitch in shoulder seam, 19 (21, 23) stitches along back neck, 1 stitch in shoulder seam, and 36 stitches along left front neck—93 (95, 97) stitches.

Begin rib pattern: Next row (WS) *P1, k1; repeat from*, p1.
Shape right front collar: Row 1 (RS) Rib 36, wrap next stitch and turn work (W&T).
Row 2 Rib to end.
Row 3 Rib to 2 stitches before last wrapped stitch, W&T.

Rows 4 and 6 Rib to end.
Row 5 Rib to 4 stitches before last wrapped stitch, W&T.
[Repeat Rows 3–6] 3 (4, 2) times more.
Size 6 months only: *Next row (RS) Rib to 4 stitches before last wrapped stitch, W&T.
Next row Rib to end. Repeat from* once more.
Sizes 12 and 24 months only: *Next row (RS) Rib to 2 stitches before last wrapped stitch, W&T.
Next row Rib to end. Repeat from* 0 (6) times more.
All Sizes: Next row (RS) Rib to end of row, hiding wraps when you come to them.
Shape left front collar: Row 1 (WS) Rib 36, W&T.
Row 2 Rib to end.
Row 3 Rib to 2 stitches before last wrapped stitch, W&T.
Rows 4 and 6 Rib to end.
Row 5 Rib to 4 stitches before last wrapped stitch, W&T.
[Repeat Rows 3–6] 3 (4, 2) times more.
Size 6 months only: *Next row (WS) Rib to 4 stitches before last wrapped stitch, W&T. **Next row** Rib to end. Repeat from* once more.
Sizes 12 and 24 months only: *Next row (WS) Rib to 2 stitches before last wrapped stitch, W&T. **Next row** Rib to end. Repeat from* 0 (6) times more.
All Sizes: Next row (WS) Rib to end of row, hiding wraps when you come to them.
Work 1 row even in rib. Bind off.
Sew edges of right and left front collar to bound-off stitches at center front, lapping right over left.
Set in sleeves. Sew side and sleeve seams.

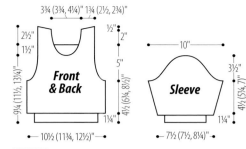

JOSEPH

Note

Carry yarn along side of work until you need it again. To avoid long strands, catch the yarn once around the working yarn of another color. Since some colors are used over an odd number of rows, working with circular needles will minimize cutting and tying on new colors. If the color needed is waiting on the other edge of the piece, slide the knitting to the other end of the circular needle, and work from that side. This will mean occasionally working 2 consecutive RS or WS rows.

Stripe pattern

* 1 Row A, 1 row B, 2 rows C, 1 row B, 1 row A, 2 rows MC, 1 row C, 2 rows MC. Repeat from*(11 rows) for Stripe Pattern.

Back

With smaller needles and MC, cast on 53 (61, 65) stitches. Work in k1, p1 rib for 1¼", increasing 4 stitches evenly across last (WS) row—57 (65, 69) stitches. Change to larger needles. Work in Stripe Pattern for 32 (48, 60) rows. Piece measures approximately 5¾ (8, 9¾)" from beginning.

Shape armholes
Bind off 4 stitches at beginning of next 2 rows. Decrease 1 stitch each side every RS row 4 times—41 (49, 53) stitches. Work even until armhole measures 5", end with a WS row.
Shape neck
Next row (RS) K10 (14, 15), join 2nd ball of yarn, bind off center 21 (21, 23) stitches, work to end. Working both sides at same time, work even until armhole measures 7", end with a RS row.
Shape shoulder tabs
Next row (WS) Purl to end of left back tab; on right back tab, bind off 3 (5, 5) stitches, purl to end.
Next row (RS) Knit to end of right back tab; on left back tab, bind off 3 (5, 5) stitches, work to end. Repeat last 2 rows once more.
Next row (WS) Purl to end of left tab; bind off 4 (4, 5) stitches of right tab. Bind off remaining 4 (4, 5) stitches.

Front

Work as for back until armhole measures 3½", end with a WS row.
Shape neck and shoulder tabs
Next row (RS) K18 (22, 23), join 2nd ball of yarn and bind off center 5 (5, 7) stitches, work to end. Working both sides at same time, bind off from

Size 6 months SCHEWE Escorial (100% superwash wool; 50g; 137yds) in Light green (MC), Turquoise (A), and Purple (B); SCHEWE Bistro (superwash wool, mercerized cotton; 50g; 122yds) in Purple (C)

each neck edge 3 stitches twice, 2 stitches once—10 (14, 15) stitches each side. Work even until armhole measures same length as back to tab shaping. Shape shoulder tabs as for back (shaping left front tab a for right back, and right front tab as for left back).

Sleeves

With smaller needles and MC, cast on 33 (33, 37) stitches. Work in k1, p1 rib for 1¼", increasing 8 stitches evenly across last (WS) row—41 (41, 45) stitches. Change to larger needles. Work in Stripe Pattern, AT SAME TIME, increase 1 stitch each side (working increases into pattern), every 2nd (4th, 8th) row 2 (6, 4) times, then every 4th (6th, 10th) row 5 (1, 1) times—55 stitches. Work even until piece measures 5¾ (6½, 8¼)", end with same row in Stripe Pattern as back underarm.

Shape cap

Bind off 4 stitches at beginning of next 2 rows, then 2 stitches at beginning of next 4 rows. Decrease 1 stitch each side every RS row 5 times. Work 1 row even. Bind off 2 stitches at beginning of next 8 rows. Bind off remaining 13 stitches.

Finishing

Block pieces.

Back neckband

With RS facing, smaller needles and MC, begin at armhole edge of top of right tab, and pick up and knit 12 (16, 18) stitches along top of tab, 10 stitches along side of tab, 21 (21, 23) stitches along neck, 10 stitches along side of left tab, and 12 (16, 18) stitches along top of left tab—65 (73, 79) stitches.

Begin rib pattern: Row 1 (WS) *P1, k1, p1, knit into front, back and front of next stitch (double increase made); repeat from* 2 (3, 3) times more, *p1, k1; repeat from* to last 12 (16, 16) stitches, ending with p1, *work double increase in next stitch, p1, k1, p1; repeat from* 2 (3, 3) times more.

Rows 2, 4, 5 and 6 Work even in rib pattern.

Row 3 *P1, k1, p1, work double increase in next stitch; repeat from* 3 times more, *p1, k1; repeat from* to last 16 stitches, ending with p1, *work double increase in next stitch, p1, k1, p1; repeat from* 3 times more. Bind off in rib pattern.

Front neckband

With RS facing, smaller needles and MC, begin at armhole edge of top of left tab, and pick up and knit 12 (16, 18) stitches along top of tab, 16 stitches along side of tab, 25 (25, 27) stitches along shaped portion of neck, 16 stitches along side of right tab, and 12 (16, 18) stitches along top of right tab—81 (89, 95) stitches. Work as for back neckband.

Mark armhole on front and back 5" above underarm. Overlap back over front tabs until markers meet. Sew tab edges at armhole, removing front marker. Set in sleeve, centering top of sleeve cap at marker.

13a Stitch Heirs

In these designs we wanted to do old-fashioned 'cute' baby outfits, but in slightly heavier yarns and brighter colors than the usual powdery hues. The cardigan has the traditional baby girl look, while the pullover set is more unisex and uses Aran motifs.

Designed by Wendy Sacks

INTERMEDIATE

LOOSE FIT
PULLOVER
12 (18, 24) months

A 23 (25, 27)"
B 12 (12¾, 13¾)"
C 14½ (16, 17½)"

10cm/4"

32

26

over reverse stockinette stitch (purl on RS, knit on WS), using larger needles

1 2 **3** 4 5 6

- Light weight
- 400 (450, 500) yds

- 3.25mm/US 3 and 3.75mm/US 5 or size to obtain gauge

- 3.5mm/E-4

- one 6mm/¼"

- cable needle (cn)
- stitch holders
- stitch markers

60

3½ (4¼, 4½)" ¼"

2¼(2½, 3)"

¾(½, 0)"

5¼ (5½, 6)"

Front & Back

8¼ (9, 10)"

5 (5½, 6)"

1"

11½ (12½, 13½)"

PULLOVER

Notes

1 See *Techniques*, page 110, for SSK, SSP, Make 1 purl (M1P) and slip stitch crochet. **2** Keep 2 stitches at each edge in stockinette stitch (knit on RS, purl on WS). Work raglan decreases and sleeve increases after first 2 stitches and before last 2 stitches.

Back

With smaller needles, cast on 75 (81, 87) stitches.

Begin K3, P3 Rib pattern: Row 1 (RS) * K3, p3; repeat from*, end k3. Work 6 rows more in rib pattern as established.

Change to larger needles.

Next row (WS) P2, knit to last 2 stitches, p2.

Begin pattern: Row 1 (RS) K2, p22 (25, 28), k1, p25, k1, p22 (25, 28), k2.

Row 2 P2, k22 (25, 28), p1, k25, p1, k22 (25, 28), p2. Repeat last 2 rows 19 (21, 23) times more. Piece measures approximately 6 (6½, 7)" from beginning.

Shape raglan armholes

Bind off 4 stitches at beginning of next 2 rows.

Decrease row (RS) K2, SSP, work to last 4 stitches, p2tog, k2.

Next row P2, work to last 2 stitches, p2. Repeat last 2 rows 7 (8, 10) times more—51 (55, 57) stitches. Armhole measures approximately 2¼ (2½, 3)".

Divide for back opening

Next row (RS) K2, SSP, work 21 (23, 24) stitches, join a 2nd ball of yarn, p2tog, work to last 4 stitches, p2tog, k2. Working both sides at same time, continue working raglan armhole decreases as for back—13 (15, 16) stitches each side. Armhole measures approximately 5¼ (5½, 6)". Bind off all stitches.

Size 18 months BERNAT Berella Country Garden DK (superwash wool; 50g; 135yds) in Green (pullover on page 59) and Coral (cardigan on page 63)

Front

With smaller needles, cast on 75 (81, 87) stitches. Work in k3, p3 rib as for back. Change to larger needles.

Next row (WS) P2, k22 (25, 28), place marker (pm), k5, pm, k17, pm, k5, pm, k22 (25, 28), p2.

Begin Charts A and B: Row 1 (RS) K2, purl to marker, work Chart A over 5 stitches (increased to 9), Chart B over 17 stitches (increased to 25), Chart A over 5 stitches (increased to 9), purl to last 2 stitches, k2.

Row 2 P2, knit to marker, work Chart A over 9 stitches, Chart B over 25 stitches, Chart A over 9 stitches, knit to last 2 stitches, p2. Continue in patterns as established until piece measures same length as back to underarm. (**For sizes 18 and 24 months only** After 16 rows of Chart B have been worked a total of 4 times, work in reverse stockinette stitch over center 17 stitches.) Shape raglan armholes as for

back, AT SAME TIME, after 24 rows have been worked above underarm, and there are 45 (51, 57) stitches, shape neck as follows:

Shape neck

Next row (RS) K2, SSP, work 12 (15, 18) stitches in pattern, join a 2nd ball of yarn and bind off 13 stitches, work to last 4 stitches, p2tog, k2. Working both sides at same time, continue working raglan armhole decreases every other row, AT SAME TIME, decrease 1 stitch at each neck edge every other row 3 (6, 6) times, then every 4th row 1 (0, 1) time, work until there are 5 stitches at each shoulder, end with a WS row.

Next row (RS) K1, SSK, k2tog; on right shoulder, SSK, k2tog, k1. Work 1 row even.

Next row (RS) K1, SSK; on right shoulder, k2tog, k1. Work 1 row even. Bind off remaining 2 stitches each side.

Chart A

Begin on 5 stitches

Chart B

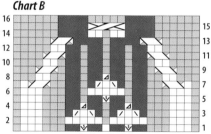

Begin on 17 stitches

Stitch Key

☐ Knit on RS, purl on WS
▨ Purl on RS, knit on WS
⊙ Yo
⊡ **Make 5** [k1, yo, k1, yo, k1] into a stitch
■ Stitches do not exist in these areas of chart
◣ SSK
◢ K2tog
◢ P3tog on WS
⧄⧄ **2/1 RPC** Slip 1 to cn, hold to back, k2; p1 from cn
⧅⧅ **2/1 LPC** Slip 2 to cn, hold to front, p1; k2 from cn
⧄⧄⧄ **2/3 RPC** Slip 3 to cn, hold to back, k2; slip first stitch from cn to left needle and purl it; k2 from cn

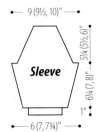

9 (9½, 10)"
5¼ (5½, 6)"
6¼ (7, 8)"
1"

Sleeve

6 (7, 7¾)"

Sleeves

With smaller needles, cast on
39 (45, 51) stitches. Work in k3, p3 rib
as for back. Change to larger needles.
Next row (WS) P2, k15 (18, 21), pm, k5,
pm, k15 (18, 21), p2.
Begin Chart A: Row 1 (RS) K2, M1P, purl to
marker, work Chart A over 5 stitches,
p15 (18, 21), M1P, k2. Continue in
pattern as established, AT SAME TIME,
increase 1 stitch each side (working
increases into reverse stockinette
stitch) every 4th (6th, 8th) row 6 (3, 1)
times, every 6th (8th, 10th) row 3 (4, 5)
times—59 (61, 65) stitches. Work even
until piece measures approximately 7¼
(8, 9)" from beginning, end with chart
row 2 (4, 4).
Shape cap
Bind off 4 stitches at beginning of next
2 rows. Decrease 1 stitch each side
every RS row 20 (21, 23) times. Bind off
remaining 11 stitches.

Finishing

Block pieces. Sew raglan sleeves to
raglan armholes of front and back. Sew
side and sleeve seams.
Neckband
With RS facing and smaller needles,
begin at left center back and pick up
and knit 75 (81, 87) stitches evenly
around neck edge.
Knit 1 row.
Work 6 rows in k3, p3 rib, working
buttonhole on third row as follows:
k2tog, yo, rib to end. Bind off all
stitches in rib. With RS facing and
crochet hook, work 1 row slip stitch
along both sides of center back opening.
Sew on button.

**Download
Free Pants
Pattern**

GO TO
knittinguniverse.com

13b Stitch Heirs

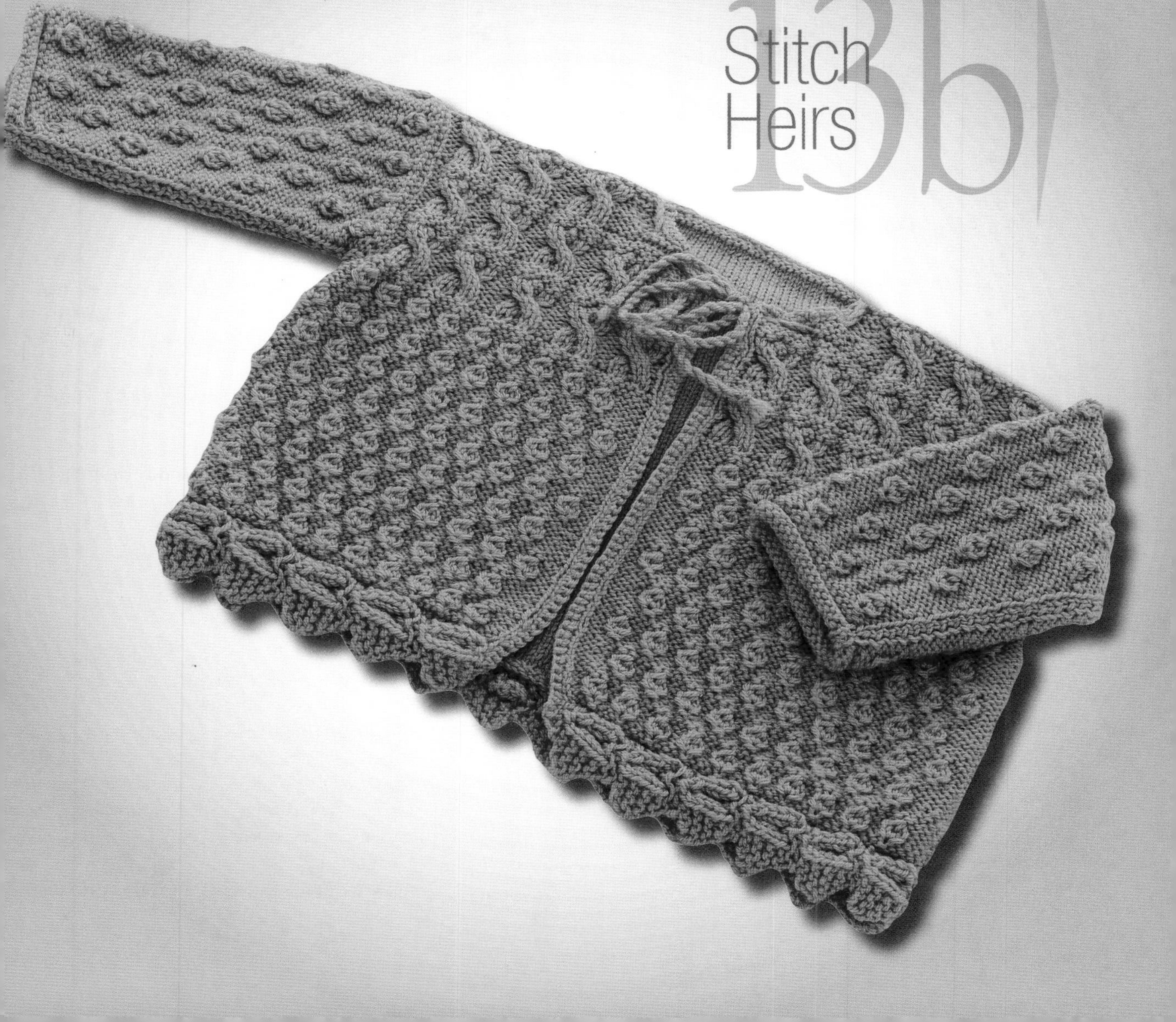

13b

Charts

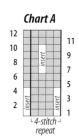

Chart A

12, 11, 10, 9, 8, 7, 6, 5, 4, 3, 2, 1

insert

4-stitch repeat

Insert

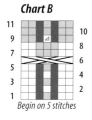

Chart B

11, 10, 9, 8, 7, 6, 5, 4, 3, 2, 1

Begin on 5 stitches

Stitch Key
☐ *Knit on RS, purl on WS*
☐ *Purl on RS, knit on WS*
■ *Stitches do not exist in these areas of chart*
⩗ *KOK K1, yo, k1 in a stitch*
◺ *P3tog on WS*

2/3 Left Increase Cable
Slip 3 to cn, hold to front, k2; slip first stitch from cn back to left needle and KOK in this stitch; k2 from cn (2 stitches increased)

INTERMEDIATE

OVERSIZED FIT

CARDIGAN
newborn (12, 18) months
A 26¼ (29, 31¾)"
B 10½ (11½, 12)"
C 11 (12½, 14)"

10cm/4"

32/32
26/24
over reverse stockinette stitch
(purl on RS, knit on WS)
using larger needle
over Chart A

1 2 **3** 4 5 6

• Light weight
• 400 (450, 500) yds

3.75mm/US 5
or size to obtain gauge

• 3.5mm/E-4

&

• cable needle (cn)
• stitch holders
• stitch markers

CARDIGAN

Notes

1 See *Techniques*, page 110, for SSK, SSP, chain stitch, slip stitch crochet, single crochet (sc), and twisted cord.
2 Keep 2 stitches at each edge in stockinette stitch (knit on RS, purl on WS). Work sleeve increases after first 2 stitches and before last 2 stitches.

Back

Cast on 80 (88, 96) stitches.
Begin pattern: Row 1 (WS) P2, knit to last 2 stitches, p2.
Row 2 K2, purl to last 2 stitches, k2.
Repeat last 2 rows 17 (20, 23) times more, then repeat Row 1 once more. Piece measures approximately 4½ (5½, 6)" from beginning.
Shape armholes
Bind off 4 stitches at beginning of next 2 rows—72 (80, 88) stitches. Keeping first and last 2 stitches in stockinette stitch, work 34 rows even. Armhole measures approximately 4½". Bind off all stitches.

Left Front

Cast on 40 (44, 48) stitches.
Next row (WS) P2, knit to last 2 stitches, p2.

Begin Chart A: Row 1 (RS) K2, p4 (2, 4), place marker (pm), work Chart A to last 5 (3, 5) stitches, end p3 (1, 3), k2.
Row 2 P2, k3 (1, 3), work Chart A between markers, end k4 (2, 4), p2.
Continue in pattern as established until 12 rows of chart have been worked 3 (3, 4) times, then work first 6 rows of chart 0 (1, 0) time more. Piece measures approximately 4½ (5½, 6)" from beginning.
Shape armhole
Next row (RS) Bind off 4 stitches, knit to end (removing markers)—36 (40, 44) stitches.
*** Begin Chart B: Row 1** (WS) P2, k1, [work Chart B over 5 stitches, k3] 3 (3, 4) times, work Chart B over 5 stitches, k2 (6, 2), p2.
Row 2 K2, p2 (6, 2), [work Chart B over 5 stitches, p3] 3 (3, 4) times, work Chart B over 5 stitches, p1, k2.
Continue in pattern as established through chart row 11.
Next row (RS) Knit.
Repeat from * once more. Armhole measures approximately 3".
Shape neck
Next row (WS) Bind off 4 (5, 6) stitches,

KOK INCREASE (k1-yo-k1)

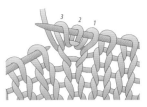

1 Knit 1, leaving stitch on left needle. *2* Bring yarn to front and over needle. *3* Knit into the stitch again.

Completed increase: 3 stitches from 1 stitch.

p1 (2 stitches on right needle), k13 (12, 11), pm, [work Chart B over 5 stitches, k3] 1 (1, 2) times, work Chart B over 5 stitches, k2 (6, 2), p2.

Next row Work chart pattern to marker, p13 (12, 11), k2.

Next row (WS) Bind off 4 (5, 6) stitches, p1, knit to marker, work chart pattern to end.

Next row Work chart pattern to marker, p7 (5, 3), p2tog, k2. Continue to decrease 1 stitch at end of RS rows 3 times more—24 (26, 28) stitches. Work 1 row even. Bind off.

Right Front

Cast on 40 (44, 48) stitches.

Next row (WS) P2, knit to last 2 stitches, p2.

Begin Chart A: Row 1 (RS) K2, p3 (1, 3), pm, work Chart A to last 6 (4, 6) stitches, end p4 (2, 4), k2. Continue in pattern as established until 12 rows of chart have been worked 3 (3, 4)

times, then work first 6 rows of chart 0 (1, 0) time more.

Next row (RS) Knit.

Shape armhole

Begin Chart B: Row 1 (WS) Bind off 4 stitches, p1, k2 (6, 2), [work Chart B over 5 stitches, k3] 3 (3, 4) times, work Chart B over 5 stitches, k1, p2—36 (40, 44) stitches. Continue in pattern as established until armhole measures same length as left front to neck, end with Row 11 of Chart B.

Shape neck

Next row (RS) Bind off 4 (5, 6) stitches, knit to end. Continue to shape neck to correspond to left front by binding off 4 (5, 6) stitches at beginning of next RS row. Then work k2, SSP at beginning of next 4 RS rows. Work 1 row even. Bind off.

Sleeves

Cast on 43 stitches. Beginning with a purl row, work 5 rows in stockinette stitch.

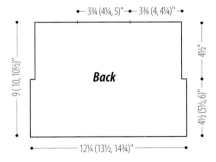

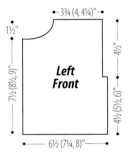

Chart C

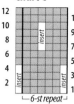

12 11
10   9
 8   7
 6   5
 4   3
 2   1

└─ 6-st repeat ─┘

Insert

Chart D

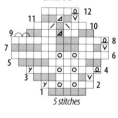

5 stitches

Next row (RS) K2, purl to last 2 stitches, k2.
Next row P2, knit to last 2 stitches, p2.
Begin Chart C: Row 1 (RS) K2, p1, work Chart C to last 3 stitches, end p1, k2. Continue in chart pattern as established, AT SAME TIME, increase 1 stitch each side (working increases into chart pattern) every 6th row 6 (3, 0) times, every 8th row 0 (3, 6) times. Work even until piece measures approximately 5½ (6¼, 7)" from beginning (with edge rolled), end with chart row 6 (12, 6)—55 stitches. Bind off.

Finishing

Block pieces. Sew shoulders. Set in sleeves. Sew side and sleeve seams.
Leaf edging
Cast on 5 stitches. Repeat Rows

1–12 of Chart D until edging fits along lower edge of cardigan.
Sew in place.
Crocheted border
With RS facing and crochet hook, beginning at right front edge, join yarn to cast-on stitches of leaf edging, chain 1 and work slip stitch evenly along right front edge, neck edge and left front edge to bound-off stitches of leaf edging. Chain 1, turn and work 1 row sc, working 2 sc at corners.
Neck ties
Make 2 twisted cords, each 14" long (finished length). Sew ties to WS at each shoulder. Weave ties around neck edge to center fronts.

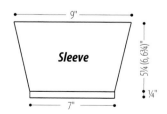

9"

Sleeve

5¼ (6, 6¾)"

¼"

7"

Download Free Pants Pattern

GO TO
knittinguniverse.com

66

14

Baby
Bunting

After spending a weekend with Kaffe Fassett's Family Album, Michele decided to make 'one of those sweaters with millions of colors.' She used a photocopy of a Southwestern mosaic as a starting point, then turned the chart and saw that if the pattern were done side to side, there would be only two colors per row.

Designed by Michele Maks

Baby Bunting

INTERMEDIATE

Size 0–6 months
to fit chest measuring 19"

10cm/4"

24

24

• in stockinette stitch (knit on RS,
purl on WS), using larger needles

1 2 **3** 4 5 6

• Light weight
MC • 615 yds
A, B, C • 246 yds each

• 3.5mm/US 4 and 4mm/US 6, or size
to obtain gauge

• 4mm/G-6

&

• stitch holders
• 20" zipper
• 1½ yds cording for drawstring
• ¼ yd nylon fabric for drawstring casings
• sewing needle & thread

Notes
1 See *Techniques*, page 110, for SSK, single crochet, 3-needle bind-off, and setting in zipper. **2** Bunting body is worked side to side. Yoke and bottom pieces are picked up along longer sides of body piece.

Body
With larger needles and MC, cast on 85 stitches. Work Chart A for 181 rows. Piece measures approximately 30¼" from beginning. Bind off all stitches with MC.

Sleeves
With smaller needles and MC, cast on 31 stitches. Work in k1, p1 rib for 2", end with a RS row.
Next row (WS) [Purl into front and back of next stitch] 30 times, p1—61 stitches. Change to larger needles. Work Chart A until piece measures 6½" from beginning. Bind off all stitches with MC.

Hood
With smaller needles and MC, cast on 85 stitches. Work in k1, p1 rib for 2", end with a WS row. Change to larger needles. Work Chart A until piece

measures 8½" from beginning. Bind off all stitches with MC.

Yoke
With RS facing, larger needles and MC, pick up and knit 181 stitches evenly along one long edge of body.
Next row (WS) P1, [p2tog] 4 times, [p1, p2tog] 55 times, [p2tog] 3 times, p1—119 stitches.
Divide for fronts and back
Begin Chart B: Row 1 (RS) Work first stitch of chart, then work 14-stitch repeat twice (29 stitches for right front), with B, bind off 2 stitches (for underarm), work 14-stitch repeat of chart 4 times (57 stitches for back, including stitch remaining on right needle after bind-off), with B, bind off 2 stitches (for underarm), work 14-stitch repeat of Chart B twice (29 stitches for left front).
Next row (WS) Work row 2 of chart over 29 stitches of left front and place remaining stitches on hold.

Left Front
Continue in pattern as established through chart row 21, then work rows 1–4 once more. Armhole measures approximately 4".

Page 67 PLYMOUTH Emu Superwash DK (wool; 50g; 123yds) in Turquoise (MC), Light Brown (A), Rust (B), and Orange (C)

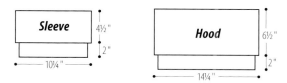

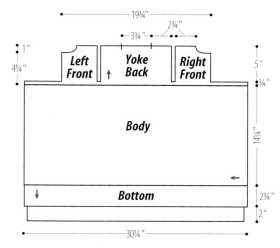

↑ *direction of knitting*

Shape neck

Next row (WS) Bind off 10 stitches (neck edge), work in pattern to end.

Next row Work to last 3 stitches, k2tog, k1. Work 1 row even.

Next row (RS) With MC, knit to last 3 stitches, k2tog, k1—17 stitches.

Next row With MC, purl. Place stitches on hold.

Right Front

With WS facing, join yarns and, beginning with row 2 of Chart B, work through chart row 21, then work rows 1-3 once more.

Shape neck

Next row (RS) Bind off 10 stitches (neck edge), work in pattern to end. Work 1 row even.

Next row (RS) K1, SSK, work in pattern to end. Work 1 row even.

Next row (RS) With MC, k1, SSK, knit to end—17 stitches.

Next row With MC, purl. Place stitches on hold.

Back

With WS facing, join yarns and work Chart B, beginning with row 2, through chart row 21, then work rows 1-7 once more. Work 2 rows with MC. Place stitches on hold.

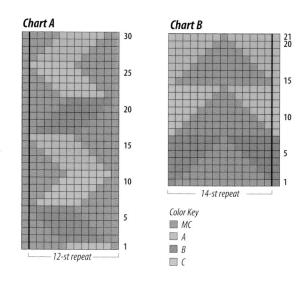

Color Key
- MC
- A
- B
- C

Chart C

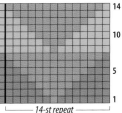

14-st repeat

Color Key
- ☐ MC
- ☐ A
- ☐ B
- ☐ C

Bottom

With RS facing, larger needles and MC, pick up and knit 181 stitches along other long edge of body. Purl 1 row with MC, increasing 2 stitches evenly— 183 stitches. Work 14 rows of Chart C. Knit 1 row with MC. Change to smaller needles. With MC, work in k1, p1 rib for 2". Bind off all stitches in rib.

Finishing

Block pieces. Join shoulders, using 3-needle bind-off. Sew sleeves into armholes. Sew sleeve seams. Fold hood in half and sew one-half of bound-off edge to other half of bound-off edge. Sew hood around neck edge, with seam at center back, and leaving 1" of ribbing extending beyond front edge. Sew seam of bottom piece. With crochet hook and MC, work 1 row of firm, even single crochet along each front edge.

Sew drawstring casing

Cut a 3" x 31" piece of nylon for bottom drawstring casing. Sew a ½" hem on both short ends. Fold nylon in half lengthwise, and with RS together, sew along long edge to form a tube. Repeat process with a 3" x 15" piece of nylon for hood drawstring. The drawstring casings, which will be inserted into bottom and hood ribbings during assembly, allow the drawstring to move more easily and protect the ribbing from wear.

Place drawstring casing inside hood rib; fold rib inward, enclosing drawstring casing and sew rib in place. Place bottom drawstring casing inside bottom rib; fold rib inward, enclosing drawstring casing and sew rib in place. Thread drawstrings through casings. Knot at ends. Fold sleeve rib inward and sew in place.

Begin at the top edge and pin the zipper in place, pinning along both fronts and making sure that your patterns line up. Pin the zipper along edge until the bottom seam is reached.

With matching sewing thread, sew zipper along single crochet border with a backstitch, taking care that the zipper teeth are not too close to the crocheted edge.

Amish
Baby
Stockings

15

15

A baby gift knit by Mary Miller in 1940 for Lizbeth Upitis' older brother inspired thes stockings. The originals were very firm—knit at 10 stitches to the inch on 000 needles.

Designed by Lizbeth Upiti

Amish Baby Stockings

INTERMEDIATE

Newborn to 6 months (6–12 months)
Leg circumference approximately 6 (6½)"
Foot and toe length approximately 4 (5)"

10cm/4"

44/40

35/31

• over stockinette stitch
(knit every round)

 2 3 4 5 6

Super fine weight
MC • 100 (115) yds
CC • 50 (95) yds

Set of five 2.25mm/US 1 (2.75mm/US 2)

Notes

1 See *Techniques*, page 110, for SSK and Make 1 (M1). **2** When using yarn with long color changes, you need not change yarns every four rounds. Simply work 10 repeats of Scallop pattern with CC. For a matched pair, begin color changes at the same place on both socks. **3** Slip stitches purlwise with yarn at WS of work.

Scallop pattern (over a multiple of 9 stitches)
Round 1 * K1, yo, k2, k2tog, SSK, k2, yo; repeat from*. **Round 2** Knit. Repeat Rounds 1–2 for Scallop pattern.

❶ Leg

With MC, cast on 54 stitches. Distribute stitches on four dpns (14/13/14/13; as shown in 1a) and join, being careful not to twist. Purl one round.
Work in Scallop pattern for 24 rounds, alternating 4 rounds of MC and 4 rounds of CC.
Knit 2 rounds.
Calf shaping
Decrease round * K1, SSK, work to last 3 stitches in round, k2tog, k1.
Knit 3 rounds.
Repeat decrease round every 4th round

6 more times—40 stitches. Rearrange stitches (10/10/10/10; as shown in 1b) and work even for 1". Cut MC.

❷ Heel Flap

With CC, k10, turn work. **Next row** (WS) * Slip 1, p19 (all onto one needle). turn. **Next row** (RS) Slip 1, k19. Repeat last 2 rows 4 times more. Work WS row.

❸ Turn Heel

Row 1 (RS) Slip 1, k11, SSK, k1, turn.
Row 2 Slip 1, p6, p2tog, p1, turn.
Row 3 Slip 1, k7, SSK, k1, turn.
Row 4 Slip 1, p8, p2tog, p1, turn.
Row 5 Slip 1, k9, SSK, k1, turn.
Row 6 Slip 1, p10, p2tog, p1, turn
Row 7 Slip 1, k11, SSK, do not turn—13 stitches.

❹ Gusset

Next round (RS) With same needle, pick up and knit 6 stitches along left edge of heel flap, M1 in strand between heel flap and instep stitches (4a); with next 2 needles, knit 20 instep stitches; with fourth needle, M1 in strand between instep stitches and heel flap, pick up and knit 5 stitches along right edge of heel flap (4b), knit last edge stitch together with first heel flap stitch,

REGIA (wool, polyamide) Royal Blue (MC) with Standard Color (CC) OR Red (MC)
with Mini-Ringel Color (CC)

WORKING WITH 5 DOUBLE-POINTED NEEDLES (DPNS)

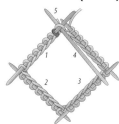

Cast stitches onto 1 dpn. Rearrange stitches on 4 dpns. Make sure stitches are not twisted. Place a marker between first and second stitch of first needle to mark beginning of round.
With a 5th dpn, work all stitches from first dpn. Use that empty dpn to work the stitches from the 2nd dpn. Continue in this manner to end of round.

knit 6 heel flap stitches from first needle—46 stitches (13/10/10/13; as shown in 4c).
Knit 1 round. Cut CC.

⑤ *Shape gusset*
Round 1 With MC, knit until 3 stitches remain on first needle, k2tog, k1; with next 2 needles, knit 20 instep stitches; with fourth needle, k1, SSK, knit across needle.
Knit 3 rounds. Repeat last 4 rounds 2 more times—40 stitches total.

Foot
Knit 24 rounds—2¼ (2½)". Cut MC.

Toe
With CC.
Knit one round.
First decrease round [K8, k2tog] on each needle.
Knit 1 round.
Second decrease round [K2, k2tog, k5] on each needle.
Continue offsetting the k2togs as you work decrease rounds as follows: Work decreases every other round twice then every round 4 times—8 stitches.
Cut yarn and run tail through remaining 8 stitches; pull tightly and secure.
Sew in ends, lightly block the lace cuff.

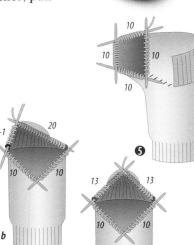

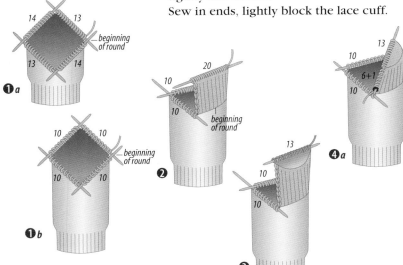

73

Here's a simple pattern ideal for churning out pairs and pairs of socks. In just a few hours, this design will give you a pair perfect for gift giving. Using several weights of yarn will give you options. Follow our details for getting started.

Designed by Diane Soucy

Playful Pairs

EASY+

Newborn to 2 years

The size of your socks will vary depending on the yarn and needles used

26–16
over stockinette stitch (knit all rounds)

1 **2·3·4** 5 6

Fine–Medium weight

• A ball of your favorite yarn or approximately 75 yards from a previous baby project

• four any size suitable for the yarn chosen

Notes

1 See *Techniques*, page 110, for SSK. *2* Slip stitches purlwise with yarn at WS of work.

SOCK

① Leg

Cast on 24 stitches onto a double-pointed needle. Arrange stitches with 8 stitches on each of 3 needles (8/8/8). Join, being careful not to twist stitches. Work in k1, p1 rib for 16 rounds. Knit 3 rounds.

② Heel Flap

Next row Knit 6, turn work.

Next row Purl back over these 6 stitches and next 6 stitches (12 stitches for heel). Divide remaining 12 stitches onto 2 needles to hold for instep.

Work back and forth on heel stitches as follows: *Row 1* (RS) Slip 1, k11. *Row 2* Slip 1, p11. Repeat Rows 1 and 2 five times more.

Turn Heel

③ *Row 1* (RS) K7, k2tog, k1, turn.

Row 2 (WS) Slip 1, p3, p2tog, p1, turn.

Row 3 Slip 1, k4, k2tog, k1, turn.

Row 4 Slip 1, p5, p2tog, p1—8 stitches.

Gusset

④ₐ Slip 12 instep stitches onto 1 needle, then using a free needle, k4 heel stitches, using another free needle, k4 other heel stitches, and using same needle, pick up and knit 6 stitches along side of heel. Using another needle, k12 instep stitches. Using another needle, pick up and knit 6 stitches along other side of heel, and using this same needle, knit remaining 4 heel stitches—32 stitches (10/12/10). Beginning of round is now center of heel.

Shape gusset

④ᵦ *Next round* Knit.

Decrease round Knit to last 3 stitches of first needle, k2tog, k1; k12 instep stitches on 2nd needle; k1, SSK, knit to end of third needle. Repeat last 2 rounds 3 times more—24 stitches (6/12/6).

⑤ Foot

Knit 10 rounds, or until foot measures desired length to beginning of toe shaping.

⑥ Toe

Decrease round Knit to last 3 stitches of first needle, k2tog, k1; k1, SSK, knit to last 3 stitches of second needle, k2tog, k1; k1, SSK, knit to end of third needle.

Next round Knit. Repeat last 2 rounds once more. Repeat decrease round twice more—8 stitches. Break yarn. Draw yarn through remaining stitches, gather together and secure yarn to WS.

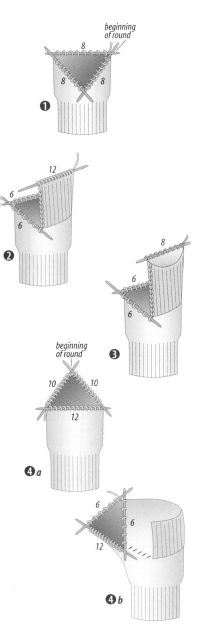

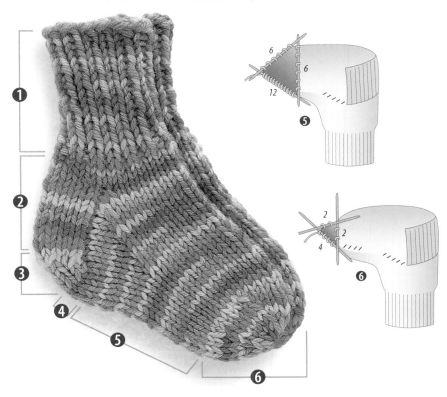

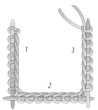

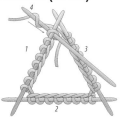

WORKING WITH 4 DOUBLE-POINTED NEEDLES (DPNS)

Cast stitches onto 1 dpn.
1 Rearrange stitches on 3 dpns. Check carefully that stitches are not twisted around a dpn or between dpns before beginning to work in rounds.
2 With a 4th dpn, work all stitches from first dpn. Use that empty dpn to work the stitches from the 2nd dpn. Use that empty dpn to work the stitches from the 3rd dpn—one round completed.

Place a marker between first and second stitch of first needle to mark beginning of round.
Notice that you work with only 2 dpns at a time. As you work the first few rounds, be careful that the stitches do not twist between the needles.

Lace medallions often grow into doilies, tablecloths, and shawls. This baby bonnet, backed with a round medallion, is a pretty way to start small.

Designed by Harriet Adams

Bonnie Bonnet

INTERMEDIATE +

Sizes 3 (6, 12) months
Circumference 12 (13, 14)"
around the face

10cm/4"

42/40/38

30/28/26

• over stockinette stitch (knit on RS, purl on WS), using larger needles

 2 3 4 5 6

• Super Fine weight
• 225 yds

Four each
3 months • 2.25mm/US 1 and 2.75mm/US 2
6 months • 2.75mm/US 2 and 3.25mm/US 3
12 months • 3.25mm/US 3 and 3.5mm/US 4
or size to obtain gauge

• 2.25mm/B (2.75mm/C, 3.25mm/D)

&

• 20 (22, 24)" ribbon

Notes

1 See *Techniques*, page 110, for SSK, Make 1 purl (M1P), single crochet (sc), chain stitch (ch st), and slip stitch (sl st).
2 Use slip knot circular cast-on (see page 37) for center star EXCEPT begin Step 2 with a k1.

BONNET

Center Star

With smaller needles, cast on 7 stitches, divided over 3 needles (2/3/2). Join and work 26 rounds of Center Star Chart—84 stitches. Change to larger needles. Turn work.
Next row (WS) Bind off 1 stitch, purl until there are 11 stitches on right needle, [M1P, p20] 3 times, M1P, p12, turn work—87 stitches (25/38/24).

Sides

Working back and forth in rows, work rows 1–16 of Quatrefoil Chart twice, then work rows 1–8 once more. Sides measure approximately 3¾ (4, 4¼)".

Picot edging

Work 4 rows in stockinette stitch.
Eyelet row (RS) *K2tog, yo; repeat from*, end k1. Work 4 more rows in stockinette stitch. Bind off loosely.

Finishing

Turn hem to WS along eyelet row and sew in place. With RS facing and crochet hook, work sc along lower edge of bonnet. Work 1 more row sc.
Picot edge: Next row *Work 3 sc, ch 3, work sl st into first ch; repeat from*. Sew a 10 (11, 12)" piece of ribbon to each front corner of bonnet.

Quatrefoil Chart

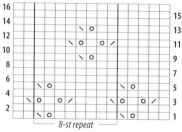

8-st repeat

Center Star Chart

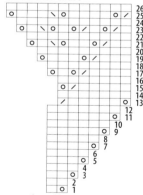

1-st to 12-st repeat

Stitch Key

☐	Knit on RS, purl on WS
⊙	Yo
╱	K2tog
╲	SSK

18
Baby Block
Afghan

Since most kids seem to hold onto their blankies for years, this one is generously sized.
Size it up or down by adding or eliminating diamonds and chevron panels.

Designed by Lily M. Chin

Baby Block Afghan

INTERMEDIATE

Finished Measurements
Blocked
45" x 62"

10cm/4"

34

17

• over garter stitch (knit every row)

1 2 3 **4** 5 6

• Medium weight
A • 1500 yds
B & C• 500 yds each

• 4mm/US 6, or size to obtain
gauge, 60cm/24" long

• 3.75mm/F-5

&

• stitch markers

Notes
1 See *Techniques*, page 110, for SSK, SK2P, Make 1 (M1), pick up and knit (purl), and single crochet. **2** Slip stitches purlwise with yarn in front. **3** Use a circular needle to accommodate the large number of stitches. **4** For ease in working, mark RS of each diamond of First Diamond Row. **5** Photo shows afghan upside down.

AFGHAN
First Diamond Row
DIAMOND (make 5)
With A, cast on 55 stitches.
Row 1 (RS) Slip 1, knit to end.
Row 2 and all WS rows Slip 1, knit to end.
Row 3 Slip 1, k25, SK2P, k26.
Row 5 Slip 1, k24, SK2P, k25.
Row 7 Slip 1, k23, SK2P, k24. Continue in pattern as established, working 1 less knit stitch at each side of center SK2P on every RS row, until 3 stitches remain, end with a WS row.
Row 55 SK2P; fasten off last stitch.
First Chevron Band
With RS of diamonds facing and B, cast on 26 stitches, then pick up and knit 27 stitches along left edge of first diamond, place marker (pm), *pick up and knit 27 stitches along right edge of next diamond, pm, then 27 stitches along left edge of same diamond, pm; repeat from*twice more, pick up and knit 27 stitches along right edge of last diamond, cast on 26 stitches—268 stitches.
Row 2 Slip 1, knit to end.
Row 3 (RS) Slip 1, k2tog, *knit to 2 stitches before marker, k2tog, slip marker (sm), SSK, knit to 1 stitch before marker, M1, k1, sm, k1, M1; repeat from*twice more, knit to 2 stitches before last marker, k2tog, sm, SSK, knit to last 3 stitches, SSK, k1—264 stitches. Repeat Rows 2 and 3 twelve times more—216 stitches. Work Row 2 once more. Cut B.
Second Diamond Row
*Row 1 (RS) With A, knit to second marker (removing both markers), turn work. Work on these 54 stitches only as follows:
Row 2 and all WS rows Slip 1, knit to end.
Row 3 Slip 1, k25, k2tog, k26—53 stitches. Work Rows 4-55 of First Diamond Row. Repeat from*3 times more (knit to end of Row 1 on last repeat).

Pages 78–79 BAABAJOES NZ Woolpak 8-ply (wool; 250g; 525yds) in Yellow (A), Red (B), and Blue (C)

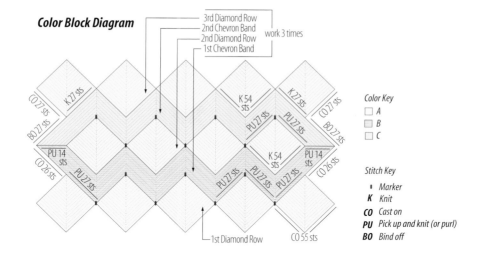

Color Block Diagram

3rd Diamond Row
2nd Chevron Band
2nd Diamond Row
1st Chevron Band

work 3 times

CO 27 sts
K 27 sts
BO 27 sts
K 54 sts
K 27 sts
CO 27 sts
PU 27 sts
PU 27 sts
BO 27 sts
PU 14 sts
CO 26 sts
PU 27 sts
K 54 sts
PU 14 sts
CO 26 sts
PU 27 sts
PU 27 sts
PU 27 sts

1st Diamond Row
CO 55 sts

Color Key
☐ A
☐ B
☐ C

Stitch Key
| Marker
K Knit
CO Cast on
PU Pick up and knit (or purl)
BO Bind off

Second Chevron Band

Row 1 (RS) With C, pick up and knit 1 stitch in edge of First Chevron Band in stitch that is closest to first diamond of Second Diamond Row, then *pick up and knit 27 stitches along right edge of diamond, pm, 27 stitches along left edge of same diamond, pm; repeat from* 3 times more (omitting last marker on last repeat), then pick up and knit 1 stitch in edge of First Chevron Band—218 stitches.

Row 2 Slip 1, knit to end, then pick up and purl 1 stitch in edge of First Chevron Band—219 stitches.

Row 3 Slip 1, *knit to 1 stitch before next marker, M1, k1, sm, k1, M1, knit to 2 stitches before next marker, k2tog, sm, SSK; repeat from* twice more, knit to 1 stitch before last marker, M1, k1, sm, k1, M1, knit to end, then pick up and knit 1 stitch in edge of First Chevron Band—222 stitches.

Repeat Rows 2 and 3 eleven times more. Work Row 2 once more—267 stitches.

Next row (RS) Bind off 27 stitches, work in pattern to end, pick up and knit 1 stitch in edge of First Chevron Band—243 stitches.

Next row Bind off 27 stitches, knit to end—216 stitches. Cut C.

Third Diamond Row

Row 1 (RS) With A, cast on 27 stitches, then k27 (removing marker), turn work. Work on these 54 stitches only as follows:

Row 2 and all WS rows Slip 1, knit to end.

Row 3 Slip 1, k25, k2tog, k26—53 stitches. Work Rows 4–55 of First Diamond Row. Work next 3 diamonds as for Second Diamond Row. Knit last 27 stitches, cast on 27 stitches. Complete last diamond as before. Work First Chevron Band, Second Diamond Row, Second Chevron Band, and Third Diamond Row twice more.

Finishing

Block.

Edging

With RS facing and crochet hook, work single crochet around entire edge of afghan, matching colors.

18b

Knitting and felting are fun for all ages. Try these little wonders for your baby or toddler and see how rewarding a simple toy can be. Fill them with craft beads and you can make a hacky-sack or juggling balls for an older child.

Designed by Kim Dolce

Felted Baby Blocks

EASY+

Small 2"
Medium 3"
Large 4"

10cm/4"

24 / 18
• before felting,
over stockinette stitch (knit on RS,
purl on WS)

1 2 3 **4** 5 6
• Medium weight
A, B, & C • 25–50 yds each per block

• 4.5mm/US 7,
or size to obtain gauge

&

• fiberfill
• yarn needle

Notes

1 See *Techniques*, page 110, for intarsia knitting. **2** Bring new color under old at color change to prevent holes. **3** Instructions are for S (M, L) blocks.

Block

With A, cast on 12 (18, 24) stitches, then with B, cast on 12 (18, 24) stitches, with a 2nd ball of A, cast on 12 (18, 24) stitches—36 (54, 72) stitches. Work in stockinette stitch for 16 (24, 32) rows, matching colors.
Next row (RS) With A, bind off 12 (18, 24) stitches, cut A and slip stitch remaining on right needle back to left needle; then with C, knit center 12 (18, 24) stitches; with A, bind off remaining 12 (18, 24) stitches. Cut A. With C, work in stockinette stitch over center stitches for 15 (23, 31) rows more. Cut C. With B, work 16 (24, 32) rows. Cut B. With C, work 16 (24, 32) rows. Bind off.

Finishing

Weave in ends. Fold sides of block and sew all but one seam. Stuff with fiberfill until full, but not firm. Sew remaining seam. Wash on hot wash/ cold rinse setting, checking every 5 minutes until block is desired size. Spin rinse. Press into shape and tumble in dryer on no-heat setting to remove remaining water. With yarn needle and desired colors, work whip stitch along each edge of block.

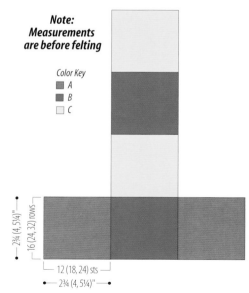

**Note:
Measurements
are before felting**

Color Key
■ A
■ B
☐ C

2¾ (4, 5¼)"
16 (24, 32) rows

12 (18, 24) sts
2¾ (4, 5¼)"

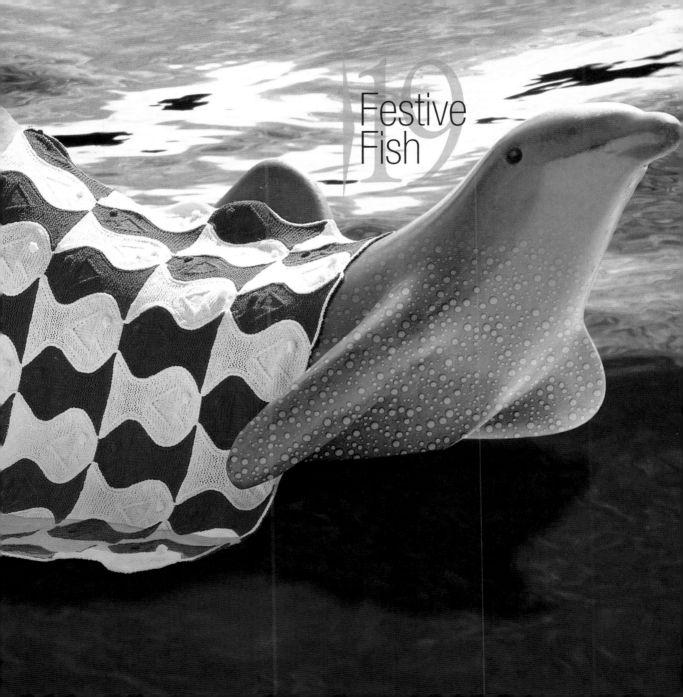

Using a fish motif, Paula presents us with a fun-to-make afghan with many color-altering prospects. As an alternative, use a family of sea tones or make each fish in a bright color.

Designed by Paula Levy

Festive Fish

Notes

1 See *Techniques*, page 110, for crochet cast-on, crochet chain stitch, SSK, SSP, and Make 1 right-slanting (M1R) and left-slanting (M1L).
2 Red and white fish are worked identically, except for chart rows 53–63.

Red fish (Make 22)

With size I hook, knitting needle, and A, crochet cast on 32 stitches. Beginning with a WS row, work 68 rows of Chart A—10 stitches. Bind off as follows:
Next row (WS) K1, k2tog, pass first stitch over (PFSO), [k1, PFSO] 4 times, SSK, PFSO, k1, PFSO. Fasten off, leaving an 8" tail for seaming.

White fish (Make 22)

With B, work as for red fish through row 52 of Chart A. Work rows 53–63 of Chart B, then rows 64–68 of Chart A. Complete as for red fish.

Finishing

Wet pieces thoroughly. Pin to measurements: 9½" long, 6½" wide at tail and 2" wide at mouth (fish will be slightly smaller in finished afghan). Smooth out to shape.

Page 83 BROWN SHEEP Nature Spun Worsted (wool; 100g; 245yds) in Red (A) and White (B)

Chart A

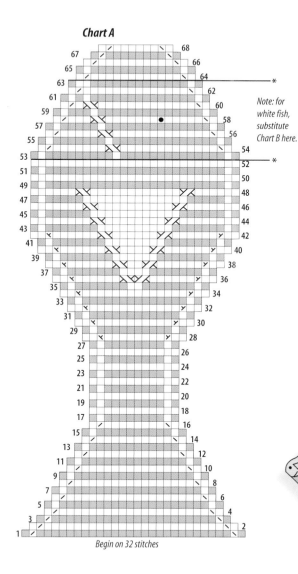

Begin on 32 stitches

Note: for white fish, substitute Chart B here.

Chart B

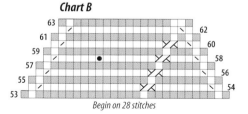

Begin on 28 stitches

Stitch Key

☐ Knit on RS, purl on WS
▨ Knit on WS
⟋ K2tog on RS, p2tog on WS
⟍ SSK on RS, SSP on WS
⟋⟍ **1/1 RT** Slip 1 to cn, hold to back, k1; k1 from cn
⟍⟋ **1/1 LT** Slip 1 to cn, hold to front, k1; k1 from cn
⊻ M1R
⊼ M1L
● **Make Bobble** Knit into front, back, front, back, front of stitch. Turn. [K5, turn] 5 times. Slip 3 together knitwise, k2tog, p3sso.

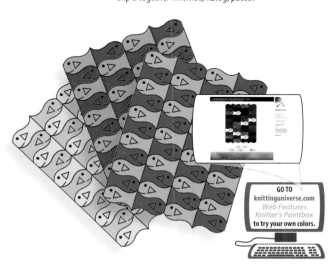

GO TO
knittinguniverse.com
Web Features
Knitter's Paintbox
to try your own colors.

Join pieces

1 Join 4 fish into a row following diagram and using overcast seam (see illustration) as follows: Hold 2 fish with RS together. Insert needle under front strand of first stitch of front piece, then from back to front under back strand of stitch on back piece, then under front strand of next stitch on front. Continue across, taking care to join complete width of mouths and tails. Seams should be firm but flexible, and invisible from RS.

2 Join rows with slip stitch. Place 2 rows face up and side by side. With size G hook and B, insert hook into purl bump or a strand at edge of white fish, then into purl bump or a strand of corresponding red fish of adjacent row. Draw up a loop. Holding yarn behind work, insert hook under another stitch on each fish. Draw loop through all stitches on hook. In same way, continue joining stitches across row, using purl bumps when available and other strands when necessary. At end of row, draw loop through final stitch. Fasten off.

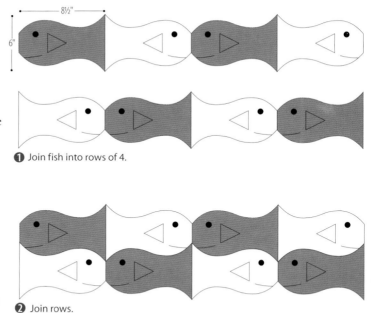

1 Join fish into rows of 4.

2 Join rows.

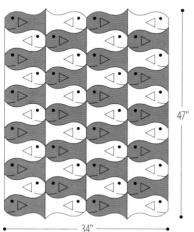

34"
47"
Finished Afghan.

Overcast seam joining fish motifs

Trim

With size G hook and B, work slip stitch around entire edge as follows: on long sides, work under both strands of chain to joining point between fish, insert hook through both pieces, draw up a loop, insert hook into first stitch of 2nd piece and draw loop through all stitches on hook. On short sides, work under purl bumps and chain 1 over peaks formed by tails; at dips near mouths, draw up a loop in each piece, then draw a loop through all 3 loops on hook. When trim is complete, cut yarn, leaving an 8" tail. Thread tail through tapestry needle, take yarn from right to left under beginning stitch, then down through last whole slip stitch.

This heirloom piece has endless using options—a baby blanket, christening shawl, kid's crib cover, or a graceful shawl. The entrelac patterning makes it an interesting design to knit, and the lace border finishes it in great style.

Designed by Diane Zangl

Enchanting Entrelac

INTERMEDIATE

Finished measurements, including border
40" x 40"

10cm/4"

28 ▦

20

• over stockinette stitch
(knit on RS, purl on WS)

1 2 3 **4** 5 6

• Medium weight
MC • 800 yds
CC • 700 yds

• 3.75mm/US 5, or size to obtain gauge,
60cm/24" long

• two 3.75mm/US 5

Note
See *Techniques*, page 110, for SSK, S2KP2, Make 1 (M1), cable cast-on, and grafting open stitches to cast-on edge.

SHAWL
With circular needle and CC, loosely cast on 120 stitches.

Work 10 base triangles
* **Row 1** (WS) P2, turn.
Row 2 and all RS rows Knit to end of base triangle being worked.
Row 3 P3, turn.
Row 5 P4, turn.
Row 7 P5, turn.
Rows 9–21 Continue to work 1 more purl stitch every WS row until there are 12 purl stitches on right needle, do not turn work after Row 21 (1 base triangle complete); repeat from * 9 times more— 10 base triangles. Turn work.

Work 1 right-side triangle
Row 1 (RS) K2, turn.
Row 2 and all WS rows Purl.
Row 3 K1, M1, SSK (1 stitch of right-side triangle together with 1 stitch of base triangle or CC rectangle), turn.
Row 5 K1, M1, k1, SSK, turn.

Row 7 K1, M1, k2, SSK, turn.
Row 9 K1, M1, k3, SSK, turn.
Rows 11–21 Continue to work 1 more knit stitch between M1 and SSK every RS row until all stitches of base triangle or CC rectangle have been worked, do not turn work after Row 21. Cut yarn.

Work 9 MC rectangles
* With RS facing and MC, pick up and knit 12 stitches along remaining side of base triangle or CC rectangle.
Row 1 (WS) P12. **Row 2** K2, [yo, k2tog] 4 times, yo, S2KP2 (last 2 stitches of rectangle together with 1 stitch from base triangle or CC rectangle). Repeat Rows 1 and 2 eleven times more. Repeat from * 8 times more—9 MC rectangles. Cut yarn.

Work 1 left-side triangle
With RS facing and CC, pick up and knit 12 stitches along remaining side of last base triangle or CC rectangle.
Row 1 (WS) P2tog, p10.
Row 2 and all RS rows Knit.
Row 3 P2tog, p9.
Row 5 P2tog, p8.
Rows 7–19 Continue to work 1 less purl stitch after p2tog every WS row until 2

88

PAGE 87 *CASCADE Key Largo (pima cotton, alpaca; 50g; 110yds) in Ecru (MC) and Natural (CC)*

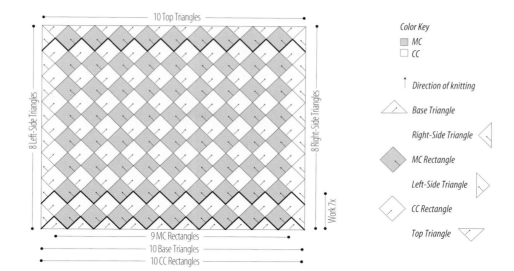

Color Key
- ☐ MC
- ☐ CC

↑ Direction of knitting

△ Base Triangle

▷ Right-Side Triangle

◇ MC Rectangle

◁ Left-Side Triangle

◇ CC Rectangle

▽ Top Triangle

10 Top Triangles

8 Left-Side Triangles

8 Right-Side Triangles

Work 7x

9 MC Rectangles
10 Base Triangles
10 CC Rectangles

stitches remain.
Row 21 P2tog, do not turn work.

Work 10 CC rectangles

With WS facing and CC, pick up and purl 11 stitches along left-side triangle—12 stitches total.
*__Row 1__ (RS) K12. **Row 2** P11, p2tog (1 stitch from CC rectangle together with 1 stitch from MC rectangle). Repeat Rows 1 and 2 eleven times more.
With WS facing, pick up and purl 12 stitches along MC rectangle; repeat from*8 times more. Repeat Rows 1 and 2 twelve times, working stitches together with right-side triangle—10 CC rectangles. Using diagram as guide, continue working entrelac pattern until there are a total of 7 rows of CC rectangles. Work right-side triangle, 9 MC rectangles, then left-side triangle.

Work 10 top triangles

*With WS facing and CC, pick up and purl 12 stitches along left-side triangle or MC rectangle—13 stitches total.
Row 1 and all RS rows Knit.
Row 2 P2tog, p10, p2tog (1 stitch of top triangle together with 1 stitch of MC rectangle or right-side triangle).
Row 4 P2tog, p9, p2tog.
Row 6 P2tog, p8, p2tog.
Rows 8–20 Continue to work 1 less purl stitch between p2tog's every WS row until 3 triangle stitches remain.
Row 22 [P2tog] twice.
Row 24 P3tog.
Repeat from*9 times more—10 top triangles. Remove needle from last loop, but do not fasten off.

Border Chart

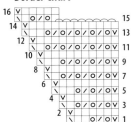

Stitch Key

- ☐ Knit on RS, purl on WS
- ⊙ Yo
- ☑ SSK (1 st of border tog with 1 picked-up st of shawl)
- ☑ K2tog
- ☑ On RS, Slip 1 knitwise with yarn in back; on WS, slip 1 purlwise with yarn in front
- ⌒ Bind off 1 stitch

Border

With RS facing, slip last loop onto dpn and with CC, pick up and knit 23 more stitches along 2 top triangles—24 stitches. With MC and 2nd dpn, cable cast on 6 stitches onto opposite end of needle.

Work 16 rows of Border Chart 3 times. *With CC, pick up and knit 24 stitches across next 2 triangles, work 16 rows of Border Chart 3 times; repeat from* around shawl. Graft open stitches to cast-on edge.

Finishing

Block piece, pinning out points of border.

21

Origami is the Japanese art of paper folding. This project extends the idea to knitted fabrics. These little bears are knit in no time with any yarn (and appropriate needles) you choose, then folded and stitched into a sweet little critter. Make one, a pair, or a pack.

Designed by Merike Saarniit

Origami Bears

EASY+

The size of your bear will vary depending on the yarn and needles used

• Any gauge

• A ball of your favorite yarn

• Any size needles suitable for the yarn chosen

&

• Stuffing

Notes

1 See *Techniques*, page 110, for loop cast-on. **2** Use loop cast-on throughout. **3** Bear can be knit with any yarn and any needle size (suitable for yarn). Choice of yarn and needle size will alter gauge and measurements of finished bear. **4** Leave long tails (approximately 8–10") when casting on and binding off, for seaming.

Bear

① Cast on 10 stitches. Knit 15 rows.

Break yarn, slide square to other end of needle.

② Cast on 10 stitches onto empty needle. Knit 15 rows, ending with both squares on same needle.
Do not break yarn.

③ ***Next row*** (RS) Knit across both squares (connecting them), cast on 1 stitch.
Next row Knit to end, cast on 1 stitch—22 stitches. Knit 8 more rows (10 rows total).

④ ***Next row*** (RS) Knit 6, cast on 7 stitches onto same needle, turn work, leaving remaining 16 stitches on needle to be worked later. Knit 7 rows on 13 stitches.
Next row (RS) Bind off 6 stitches, knit to end. Knit 7 rows more on 7 stitches (8 rows total). Bind off 7 stitches.

⑤ Rejoin yarn to stitches on needle and knit 30 rows on first 10 stitches only, leaving remaining 6 stitches on needle to be worked later. Bind off 10 stitches.

⑥ Cast on 7 stitches onto needle holding remaining 6 stitches (make slip knot, then cast on 6 more). Knit 7 rows on 13 stitches.
Next row (WS) Bind off 6 stitches, knit to end. Knit 7 rows more (8 rows total). Bind off 7 stitches.

← *Direction of knitting*
CO *Cast on*
BO *Bind off*

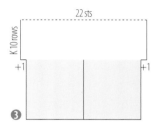

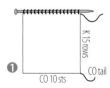

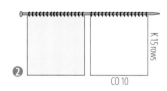

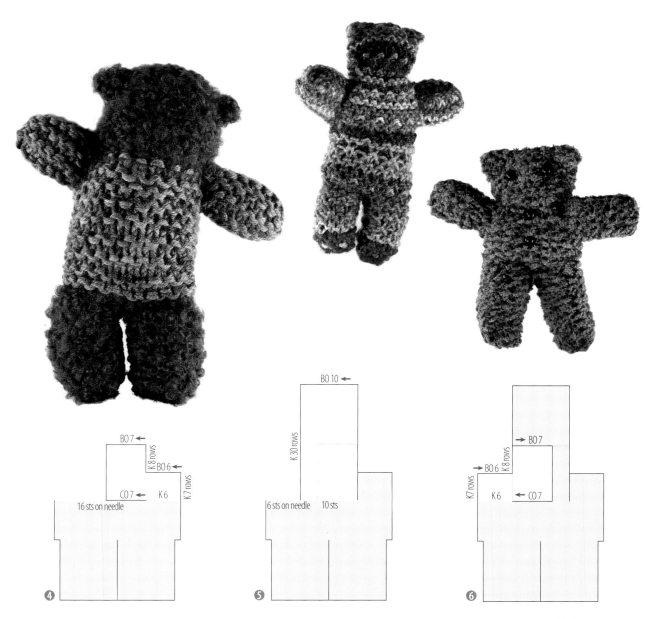

❹

BO 7 ←
K 8 rows
BO 6 ←
CO 7 ← K 6 K 7 rows
16 sts on needle

❺

BO 10 ←
K 30 rows
6 sts on needle   10 sts

❻

→ BO 7
K 8 rows
→ BO 6
K 7 rows K 6 ← CO 7

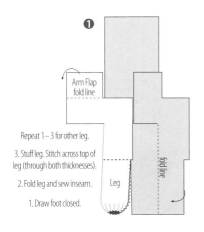

❶

Arm Flap
fold line

Repeat 1–3 for other leg.

3. Stuff leg. Stitch across top of leg (through both thicknesses).

2. Fold leg and sew inseam.

1. Draw foot closed.

fold line

Leg

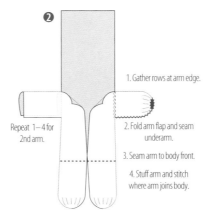

❷

Repeat 1–4 for 2nd arm.

1. Gather rows at arm edge.

2. Fold arm flap and seam underarm.

3. Seam arm to body front.

4. Stuff arm and stitch where arm joins body.

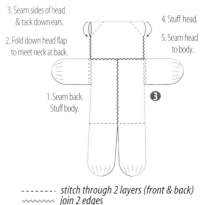

3. Seam sides of head & tack down ears.

2. Fold down head flap to meet neck at back.

1. Seam back. Stuff body.

4. Stuff head.

5. Seam head to body.

❸

- - - - - - - *stitch through 2 layers (front & back)*
〰〰〰 *join 2 edges*

OPTIONS

After stuffing, create a snout by stitching from cheek to cheek (through the stuffing).

Tie a ribbon around neck for more definition.

Finishing

Block piece.

❶ *Seam legs*

Run cast-on tail through cast-on stitches and pull tight, fold leg with wrong sides together and sew inseam of leg with same tail. Tie this yarn to yarn tail at crotch. Loosely stuff leg, then stitch across top of leg and back again (sewing through both thicknesses). Tie another knot to secure yarn. Repeat for 2nd leg.

❷ *Seam arms*

Run tail from arm bind-off through garter bumps at inside arm edge and gather tightly. Fold arm flap and seam cast-on edge to bound-off edge, then stitch the arm edge to edge of body, matching garter ridges. Loosely stuff arm. Stitch through both thicknesses where arm joins body. Secure yarn. Repeat for 2nd arm.

❸ *Seam back*

Seam back from crotch to neck, matching garter ridges. Stuff body lightly.

Seam head

Fold down head flap to meet neck at back. Starting at neck edge, seam one side to within 4 rows or so of folded end. Stitch through both layers diagonally to top of head (approximately 4 stitches in from edge), then run yarn through stitches along top of head out to point of ear and tack point to side of head. Tug yarn to round out ear. Secure yarn. Repeat for other side. Stuff head lightly. Seam back neck to body. Stitch around neck and gather to shape head. Add decorations such as beads, buttons and embroidery as desired.

After becoming fascinated by a photograph of some old, pieced-fabric puzzle balls, Susan was inspired to try knitting one. She used antique-y colors, but any scraps of sportweight yarn will do. Just knit the twelve easy pieces and sew them together. Have a ball!

Designed by Susan Douglas

Puzzle Balls

INTERMEDIATE

One size
Circumference 10–12"

10cm/4"

32
24

• over stockinette stitch (knit every round)

1 **2** 3 4 5 6

• Fine weight
• MC 55 yds
• CC 35 yds

• four 3.25mm/US 3,
or size to obtain gauge

&

• tapestry needle
• polyester stuffing

Chart Pattern

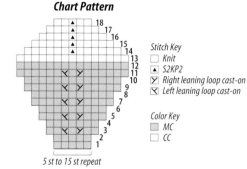

18
17
16
15
14
13
12
11
10
9
8
7
6
5
4
3
2
1

Stitch Key
☐ Knit
▲ S2KP2
☑ Right leaning loop cast-on
☒ Left leaning loop cast-on

Color Key
☐ MC
☐ CC

5 st to 15 st repeat

Note
See *Techniques*, page 110, for right and left-leaning loop cast-on and S2KP2.

Puzzle ball units (make 12)
With MC, cast on 10 stitches, leaving a 10" tail. Arrange stitches on 3 dpns (3/4/3). Join, being careful not to twist stitches. Work 18 rounds of Chart Pattern. (*Note* All increases and decreases will occur on first and third needles.) With cast-on tail, work whip-stitch in each cast-on stitch, pull stitches together tightly to gather opening closed. Cut yarn, leaving a 10" tail. Stuff unit with polyester stuffing.

Gather stitches at top as follows: Using the tapestry needle, run yarn end through stitches. Do not pull it closed yet. Starting with first stitch of last round, use tapestry needle to pull gently on front loop of stitch to tighten last stitch of second-to-last round. Now go to second stitch on last round and gently pull on front loop until first loop of round is tidy. Pull on third stitch (which tightens second stitch), and on around. Pull gathering thread end to tighten last loop. Thread yarn end through first 4 stitches again and secure it. Don't cut yarn yet, you can use it to sew units together.

Page 95 BRUNSWICK Pomfret (wool; 50g; 175 yds)

Assemble units

Arrange units in groups of four and sew them together to form groups A, B, and C. Use overcast stitches (shown in red) then wrap them as shown leaving about ¼" between units. Secure and finish off ends.

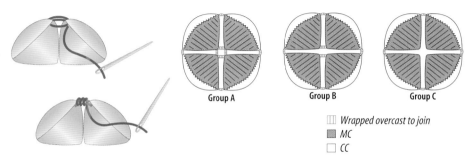

Group A   Group B   Group C

▥ Wrapped overcast to join
▨ MC
☐ CC

A and B joined, ready to slip through C.

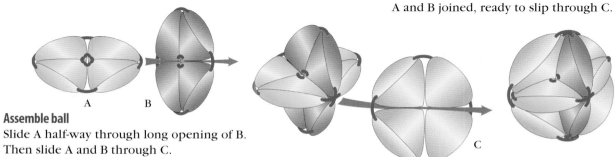

A   B

C

Assemble ball

Slide A half-way through long opening of B. Then slide A and B through C.

This lovely sage and multicolored baby afghan will surely be an heirloom piece. Knitted in blocks, the quilt-inspired design can be made larger for grown-ups.

Designed by Fiona Ellis

Quilt Block Magic

INTERMEDIATE

One size

Finished Measurements
36" x 36"

10cm/4"

28

21

• over Chart A, using MC

1 2 3 **4** 5 6

• Medium weight
MC • 1300 yds
CC • 180 yds

• 4.5mm/US 7,
or size to obtain gauge

Note See *Techniques,* page 110, for SSK, yarn over (yo) before a knit and purl stitch, and at the beginning of a row.

SQUARES (MAKE 16)

With MC, cast on 37 stitches. Purl 1 row. Work 12 rows of Chart A 4 times. Bind off.

Finishing

Steam block all squares. Sew squares together, alternating knit and purl sides as shown in diagram.

Variegated Border (Make 4)

With MC, cast on 167 stitches. Knit 1 row. Work 4 rows of Chart B 4 times, alternating MC and CC every 2 rows. With MC, knit 1 row. Bind off knitwise on WS. Sew borders around squares, extending each border 2" beyond squares on one side to allow for placement of next border (see diagram).

Joining Diagram

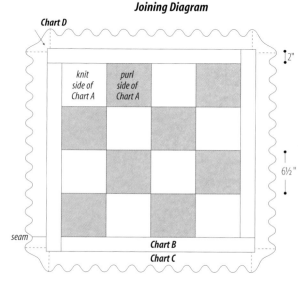

Chart A / **Chart B**

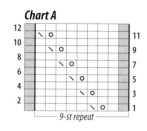

Stitch Key

☐ Knit on RS, purl on WS
▩ Purl on RS, knit on WS
↘ SSK
○ Yo
☑ Slip 1 purlwise with
yarn at WS of work

JCA/REYNOLDS Saucy (cotton; 100g; 185 yds) in 110 Moss (MC); Meadow (cotton, viscose, linen; 50g; 78 yds) in 13 Cottage Garden (CC)

Chart C

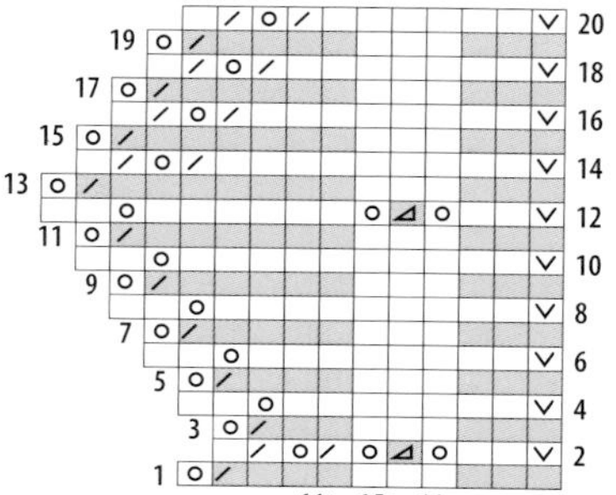

Chart C is a knitting chart, read from bottom (Row 1) to top (Row 20), with odd row numbers labeled on the left and even row numbers on the right. Marked "11 to 15 to 11 sts" below.

Row	1	2	3	4	5	6	7	8	9	10	11	12	13	14	15
20		/	○	/											∨
19	○	/		/	○	/									
18			/	○	/										∨
17	○	/			/	○	/								
16				/	○	/									∨
15	○	/				/	○	/							
14					/	○	/								∨
13	○	/					○								
12								○	◿	○					∨
11	○	/					○								
10					/	○	/								∨
9	○	/				○									
8				/	○	/									∨
7	○	/		○											
6			/	○	/										∨
5	○	/	○												
4		/	○	/											∨
3	○	/													
2		/	○	/	○	◿	○								∨
1	○	/													

11 to 15 to 11 sts

Chart D

Chart D is a knitting chart, read from bottom (Row 1) to top (Row 21), with odd row numbers on the left and even row numbers on the right. Marked "15 sts" below.

Row	1	2	3	4	5	6	7	8	9	10	11	12	13	14	15	16	17	18
21	○	/																
20			○	/			○	◿	○					∨	•			
19	○	/		○														
18			/	○	/							∨	•	•				
17	○	/			○													
16				/	○	/				∨	•	•	•					
15	○	/				○												
14					/	○	/		∨	•	•	•	•					
13	○	/					○											
12						/	○	/	∨	•	•	•	•					
11	○	/					/	○	/	∨	•	•	•	•				
10					/	○	/	∨	•	•	•	•						
9	○	/			/	○	/	∨	•	•	•	•						
8				/	○	/	∨	•	•	•	•							
7	○	/		○	/	∨	•	•	•									
6			/	○	/	∨	•	•	•									
5	○	/	○	/	∨	•	•											
4		/	○	/	∨	•	•											
3	○	/		∨	•	•												
2		/	○	/	∨	•	•											
1	○	/		•														

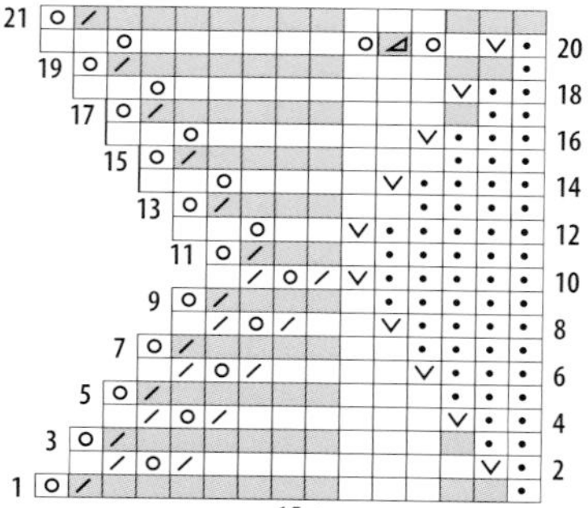

15 sts

Note for Chart D: At end of WS rows, turn work after last stitch worked, and work next RS row.

Stitch Key

- ☐ Knit on RS, purl on WS
- ▨ Purl on RS, knit on WS
- ◸ SSK
- / K2tog on RS
- / K2tog on WS
- ○ Yo
- ∨ Slip 1 purlwise with yarn at WS of work
- ◿ P3tog
- • Stitch left unworked

SCALLOPED BORDER

With MC, cast on 11 stitches. *Beginning with a WS row, work Rows 1–20 of Chart C 10 times, then work Rows 1–12 of chart once more. Work Rows 1–21 of Chart D. Work rows 14–20 of Chart C. Repeat from*3 times more. Bind off. Pin border along outside edge of variegated border, matching corners, and sew in place. Sew bound-off edge to cast-on edge.

24

Pachyderm Parade

ADVANCED

Finished measurements
36½" x 45"

10cm/4"

24

18
over stockinette stitch
(knit on RS, purl on WS)

1 2 3 **4** 5 6

Medium weight

A • 750 yds
B • 750 yds
C, D, E, F • 375 yds each

• 4mm/US 6, or size to obtain gauge

• Two 8mm/US 11 (for I-cord)

Notes

1 See *Techniques*, page 110, for mattress stitch, attached I-cord, embroidery stitches, and grafting open stitches to cast-on edge.
2 Blanket is made in separate double-knit strips which are sewn together.
3 Refer to strip charts for colors and pattern placement.

Horizontal stripe pattern

Row 1 (Side A facing) *K1C, p1E; repeat from* to end.
Row 2 (Side B facing) *K1E, p1C; repeat from* to end.
Row 3 *K1E, p1C; repeat from* to end.
Row 4 *K1C, p1E; repeat from* to end.
Repeat Rows 1–4 twice more, then work Rows 1–2 once more (14 rows total).

Vertical stripe pattern

Row 1 (Side A facing) K1C, p1E, *[k1C, p1E] 3 times, [k1E, p1C] 3 times; repeat from*, end [k1C, p1E] 4 times.
Row 2 (Side B facing) K1E, p1C, *[k1E, p1C] 3 times, [k1C, p1E] 3 times; repeat from*, end [k1E, p1C] 4 times.
Repeat Rows 1 and 2 six times more (14 rows total).

DOUBLE KNITTING

• Double knitting is simple if you think of the fabric as having two "right" sides. All the knit stitches in a row make up one layer of the fabric; the purl stitches in the same row form the "wrong" side of the other layer. Both layers are formed at the same time.
• Knit the stitches of the side that is facing you at any given

Side A facing

1. Bring both yarns to back, k1 stitch from Side A with MC.

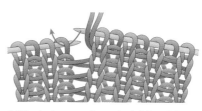

2. Bring both yarns to front, p1 stitch from Side B with CC (k1/p1 pair completed). Repeat Steps 1 and 2.

Page 101 UNGER Aries (acrylic, wool; 100g; 180yds) in Gold (A), Gray (B), White (C), Light Green (D), Medium Green (E), and Pink (F)

time (Side A or B) and purl the stitches for the opposite layer.

• Think of the stitches as being in pairs: one knit and one purl. Since the motifs are reversible, if the knit in a pair is MC, the purl will be CC, or vice versa.

• Cast on enough stitches for both Sides A and B at one time. Therefore, the cast-on will always be an even number of stitches.

• Cast on with one color and join the second color on the first chart row.

• When knitting, BOTH colors should be at the back of the work; when purling, BOTH colors should be at the front of the work.

• When completed, the double knit pieces will not be joined at the sides. When

sewing pieces together, use mattress stitch, going in ½ stitch on each side. Seam each layer separately.

• To join a color in the middle of a row, knit and purl with opposite colors. Before joining a new color, a k1/p1 pair in the old color must be completed.

• All charts are read from right to left since charts are worked from the RS.

• An ordinary bind-off is not suitable for double knitting. Use the following bind-off instead: K1, p1, * k1, pass first stitch over next 2 stitches, p1, pass first stitch over next 2 stitches; repeat from * to end. Fasten off.

Side B facing

1. Bring both yarns to back, k1 stitch from Side B with CC.

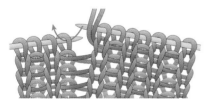

2. Bring both yarns to front, p1 stitch from Side A with MC (k1/p1 pair completed). Repeat Steps 1 and 2.

Changing colors in center of row for motifs

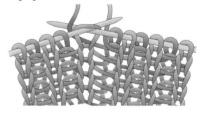

After a k1/p1 pair has been completed, work the next k1/p1 pair using the opposite colors.

BLANKET

Heart Strip (Make 4)

With A, cast on 30 stitches. Join C. **_Begin Heart Strip Chart: Row 1_** (Side A facing) *K1A, p1C; repeat from*to end.
Row 2 (Side B facing) *K1C, p1A; repeat from*to end.
Row 3 [K1A, p1C] 7 times, k1C, p1A, [k1A, p1C] 7 times.
Row 4 [K1C, p1A] 6 times, [k1A, p1C] 3 times, [k1C, p1A] 6 times. Continue in chart pattern as established through row 56, then repeat rows 1–56 four times more. Bind off.

Elephant Strip 1

With A, cast on 70 stitches. Using A and C, work 14 rows of Triple Heart Chart. Work 14 rows of Horizontal Stripe Pattern. With B and D, work 42 rows of Straight Trunk Elephant Chart, working right-facing elephant on Side A and left-facing elephant on Side B.
With D and C, work 14 rows of Triple Heart Chart.
With B and F, work 28 rows of Baby Elephant Chart, working left-facing elephant on Side A and right-facing elephant on Side B.
Work 14 rows of Vertical Stripe Pattern. With B and A, work 42 rows of Hooked Trunk Elephant Chart, working right-facing elephant on Side A and left-facing elephant on Side B.
With A and C, work 14 rows of Triple Heart Chart.
With B and D, work 28 rows of Baby Elephant Chart, working left-facing elephant on Side A and right-facing elephant on Side B.
Work 14 rows of Horizontal Stripe Pattern. With B and F, work 42 rows of Tucked Trunk Elephant Chart, working right-facing elephant on Side A and left-facing elephant on Side B.
With F and C, work 14 rows of Triple Heart Chart. Bind off.

Elephant Strip 2

Work as for Elephant Strip 1, following Strip 2 chart for colors and patterns.

Elephant Strip 3

Work as for Elephant Strip 1, following Strip 3 chart for colors and patterns.

Finishing

Sew strips together with Side A of all

Heart Strip

Side B

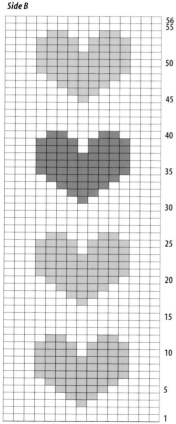

Side A

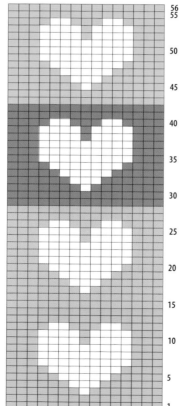

Color Key ☐ A ■ B ☐ C ☐ D ■ E ☐ F

Elephant Strip 3

Side B   Side A

Elephant Strip 2

Side B   Side A

Elephant Strip 1

Side B   Side A

strips facing, following Joining Diagram for placement of strips.

I-Cord edging

With double-pointed needles and 2 strands B held together, work 3-stitch attached I-cord around blanket, picking up stitches through both thicknesses. Graft stitches to cast-on edge. Lightly steam blanket on both

sides. Cut three 10" strands of matching yarn for each elephant's tail. Thread yarn through one layer of fabric so that there are six strands. Divide ends into 3 groups of 2 strands each and braid. Tie a knot and trim ends. If desired, use embroidery (lazy daisy stitch or chain stitch) to add details.

Joining Diagram   *Side A facing*

Heart Strip	Elephant Strip 3	Heart Strip	Elephant Strip 2	Heart Strip	Elephant Strip 1	Heart Strip

Triple Heart Chart

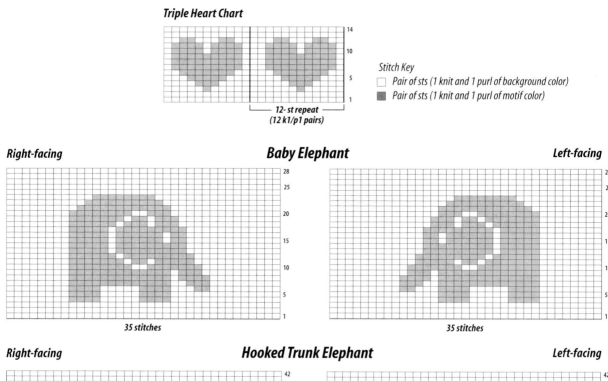

14
10
5
1

Stitch Key

☐ Pair of sts (1 knit and 1 purl of background color)
■ Pair of sts (1 knit and 1 purl of motif color)

12- st repeat
(12 k1/p1 pairs)

Baby Elephant

Right-facing

28
25
20
15
10
5
1

35 stitches

Left-facing

28
25
20
15
10
5
1

35 stitches

Hooked Trunk Elephant

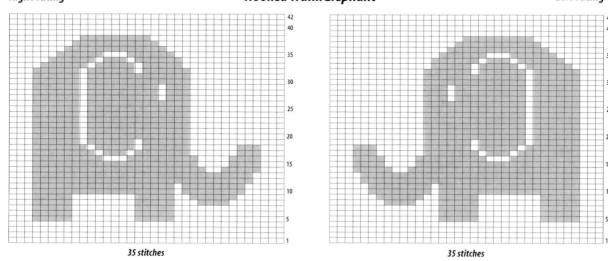

Right-facing

42
40
35
30
25
20
15
10
5
1

35 stitches

Left-facing

42
40
35
30
25
20
15
10
5
1

35 stitches

Straight Trunk Elephant

Right-facing

Left-facing

35 stitches

35 stitches

Tucked Trunk Elephant

Right-facing

Left-facing

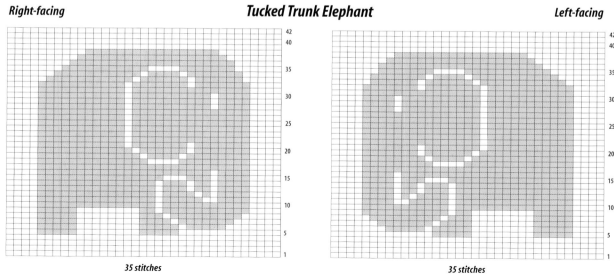

35 stitches

35 stitches

photography by Alexis Xenakis

3-NEEDLE BIND-OFF

Bind-off ridge on wrong side
1 With stitches on 2 needles, place **right sides together**. * Knit 2 stitches together (1 from front needle and 1 from back needle, as shown); repeat from * once more. *2* With left needle, pass first stitch on right needle over second stitch and off right needle.

3 Knit next 2 stitches together.
4 Repeat Steps 2 and 3, end by drawing yarn through last stitch.

Bind-off ridge on right side
Work as for ridge on wrong side, EXCEPT, with **wrong sides together**.

LOOP CAST-ON (ALSO CALLED E-WRAP CAST-ON)

 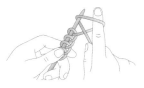

Often used to cast on a few stitches, as for a buttonhole
1 Hold needle and tail in left hand. *2* Bring right index finger under yarn, pointing toward you.

3 Turn index finger to point away from you. *4* Insert tip of needle under yarn on index finger (see above); remove finger and draw yarn snug, forming a stitch. Repeat Steps 2–4 until all stitches are on needle.

Left-slanting   *Right-slanting*
Loops can be formed over index or thumb and can slant to the left or to the right. On the next row, work **through back loop** of right-slanting loops

CABLE CAST-ON

1–2 Start with a slipknot on left needle. Insert right needle into slipknot from front. Wrap yarn over right needle as if to knit. Bring yarn through slipknot, forming a loop on right needle.

3 Insert left needle in loop and slip loop off right needle. One additional stitch cast on.

4 Insert right needle **between** the last 2 stitches. From this position, knit a stitch and slip it to the left needle as in Step 3. Repeat Step 4 for each additional stitch.

CROCHET CAST-ON

1 Leaving a short tail, make a slipknot on crochet hook. Hold hook in right hand; in left hand, hold knitting needle on top of yarn and behind hook. With hook to left of yarn, bring yarn through loop on hook; yarn goes over top of needle, forming a stitch.

2 Bring yarn under point of needle and hook yarn through loop forming next stitch. Repeat Step 2 until 1 stitch remains to cast on. Slip loop from hook to needle for last stitch.

INVISIBLE CAST-ON

A temporary cast-on
1 Knot working yarn to contrasting waste yarn. Hold needle and knot in right hand. Tension both strands in left hand; separate strands so waste yarn is over index finger, working yarn over thumb. Bring needle between strands and under thumb yarn so working yarn forms a yarn-over in front of waste yarn.

2 Holding both yarns taut, pivot hand toward you, bringing working yarn under and behind waste yarn. Bring needle behind and under working yarn so working yarn forms a yarn-over behind waste yarn.

3 Pivot hand away from you, bringing working yarn under and in front of waste yarn. Bring needle between strands and under working yarn, forming a yarn-over in front of waste yarn. Each yarn-over forms a stitch. Repeat Steps 2–3 for required number of stitches. For an even number, twist working yarn around waste strand before knitting the first row.

LONG-TAIL CAST-ON, KNIT

 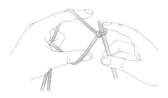 

Make a slipknot for the initial stitch, at a distance from the end of the yarn, allowing about 1½" for each stitch to be cast on.
1 Bring yarn between fingers of left hand and wrap around little finger as shown.

2 Bring left thumb and index finger between strands, arranging so tail is on thumb side, ball strand on finger side. Open thumb and finger so strands form a diamond.

3 Bring needle down, forming a loop around thumb.
4 Bring needle **under** front strand of **thumb loop**…

 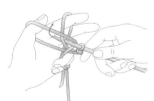  

5 …up **over index finger yarn**, catching it…

6 …and bringing it **under** the front of **thumb loop**.

7 Slip thumb out of its loop, and use thumb to adjust tension on the new stitch. One knit stitch cast on.

Repeat Steps 3–7 for each additional stitch.

SSK

1 Slip 2 stitches **separately** to right needle as if to knit.

2 Slip left needle into these 2 stitches from left to right and knit them together: 2 stitches become 1.

The result is a left-slanting decrease.

SK2P, sl 1-k2tog-psso

1 Slip 1 stitch knitwise.
2 Knit next 2 stitches together.
3 Pass the slipped stitch over the k2tog: 3 stitches become 1; the right stitch is on top.
The result is a left-slanting double decrease.

S2KP2, sl 2-k1-p2sso

1 Slip 2 stitches **together** to right needle as if to knit.

2 Knit next stitch.

3 Pass 2 slipped stitches over knit stitch and off right needle: 3 stitches become 1; the center stitch is on top.

The result is a centered double decrease.

S2KP2, sl 2-k1-p2sso ALTERNATIVE METHOD

 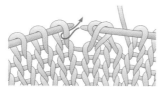  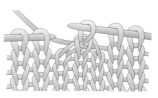

1 Slip 2 stitches together to right needle as if to knit.

2 Slip next stitch to right needle as if to knit.

3 Knit these 3 stitches together by slipping left needle into them from left to right.

4 Completed: 3 stitches become 1; the center stitch is on top.

SSP

Use instead of p2tog-tbl to avoid twisting the stitches.

1 Slip 2 stitches **separately** to right needle as if to knit.

2 Slip these 2 stitches back onto left needle. Insert right needle through their 'back loops,' into the second stitch and then the first.

3 Purl them together: 2 stitches become 1.

The result is a left-slanting decrease.

MAKE 1 LEFT (M1L), KNIT

Insert left needle from front to back under strand between last stitch knitted and first stitch on left needle. Knit, twisting strand by working into loop at back of needle.

Completed M1L knit: a left-slanting increase.

MAKE 1 RIGHT (M1R), KNIT

Insert left needle from back to front under strand between last stitch knitted and first stitch on left needle. Knit, twisting the strand by working into loop at front of the needle.

Completed M1R knit: a right-slanting increase.

MAKE 1 LEFT (M1L), PURL

 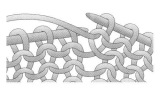

Insert left needle from front to back under strand between last stitch worked and first stitch on left needle. **Purl**, twisting strand by working into loop at back of needle from left to right.

Completed M1L purl: a left-slanting increase.

MAKE 1 RIGHT (M1R), PURL

Work as for Make 1 Right, Knit, EXCEPT **purl.**

Completed M1R purl: a right-slanting increase.

YARN OVER (yo)

Between knit stitches
Bring yarn under the needle to the front, take it over the needle to the back and knit the next stitch.

Between purl stitches
With yarn in front of needle, bring it over the needle to the back and to the front again; purl next stitch.

At beginning of a knit row
With yarn in front of needle, knit first stitch.

At beginning of a purl row
With yarn in front of needle, bring it over the needle to the back and to the front again; purl next stitch.

SLIP STITCH (sl st)

1 Insert the hook into a stitch, catch yarn, and pull up a loop.

2 Insert hook into the next stitch to the left, catch yarn and pull through both the stitch and the loop on the hook; 1 loop on the hook. Repeat Step 2.

CHAIN STITCH (ch st, ch)

1 Make a slipknot to begin.
2 Catch yarn and draw through loop on hook.

First chain made. Repeat Step 2.

SINGLE CROCHET (sc)

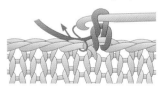  

1 Insert hook into a stitch, catch yarn, and pull up a loop. Catch yarn and pull through the loop on the hook.
2 Insert hook into next stitch to the left.

3 Catch yarn and pull through the stitch; 2 loops on hook.

4 Catch yarn and pull through both loops on hook; 1 single crochet completed. Repeat Steps 2–4.

PICK UP AND KNIT VERTICALLY

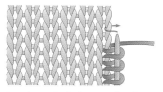

Insert needle 2 sizes smaller than garment needles **into** center of first stitch, catch yarn and knit a stitch.

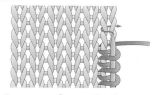

For an even firmer edge, insert needle in space **between** first and 2nd stitches.

HORIZONTALLY

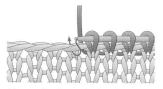

Along a horizontal edge, insert needle into center of every stitch.

PICK UP AND PURL

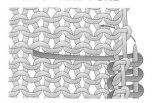

With wrong side facing and yarn in front, insert needle from back to front between first and second stitches, catch yarn, and purl.

SHORT ROWS (WRAP & TURN)

Each short row adds 2 rows of knitting across a section of the work. Since the work is turned before completing a row, stitches must be wrapped at the turn to prevent holes. Wrap and turn as follows:

Knit side
1 With yarn in back, slip next stitch as if to purl. Bring yarn to front of work and slip stitch back to left needle (as shown). Turn work.
2 With yarn in front, slip next stitch as if to purl. Work to end.

3 When you come to the wrap on a following knit row, hide the wrap by knitting it together with the stitch it wraps.

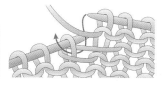

Purl side
1 With yarn in front, slip next stitch as if to purl. Bring yarn to back of work and slip stitch back to left needle (as shown). Turn work.
2 With yarn in back, slip next stitch as if to purl. Work to end.

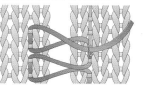

3 When you come to the wrap on a following purl row, hide the wrap by purling it together with the stitch it wraps.

MATTRESS STITCH

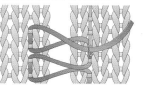

Mattress stitch seams are good all-purpose seams. They require edge stitches (which are taken into the seam allowance).
1 Place pieces side by side, with right sides facing you.
2 Thread blunt needle with matching yarn.
3 Working between edge stitch and next stitch, pick up 2 bars.
4 Cross to opposite piece, and pick up 2 bars.
5 Return to first piece, work into the hole you came out of, and pick up 2 bars.
6 Return to opposite piece, go into the hole you came out of, and pick up 2 bars.
7 Repeat Steps 4 and 5 across, pulling thread taut as you go.

INTARSIA - PICTURE KNITTING

Color worked in areas of stockinette fabric: each area is made with its own length of yarn. Twists made at each color change connect these areas.

TIPS
• Intarsia blocks are always worked back and forth, even in circular work.
• When bobbins are called for, make a **butterfly** or cut 3-yard lengths to prevent tangles.
• Work across a row and back before you untangle yarns.

Right-side row

Wrong-side row

Making a twist:
Work across row to color change, pick up new color from under the old and work across to next color change.

GRAFTING OPEN STS TO CO EDGE

Graft stitches as shown matching stitch for stitch.

TWISTED CORD

1 Cut strands 6 times the length of cord needed. Fold in half and knot cut ends together.
2 Place knotted end over a door knob or hook and right index finger in folded end, then twist cord tightly.

3 Fold cord in half, smoothing as it twists on itself. Pull knot through original fold to secure.

EMBROIDERY: CHAIN STITCH

Chain stitch can be worked 2 ways:
1 Thread the yarn into a blunt needle, or …
2 … hold yarn on the wrong side of the fabric and a crochet hook on the right side.

LAZY DAISY

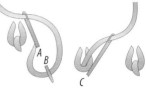

Bring needle out at A, form a loop; reinsert needle at A and bring out at B, establishing the length of the stitch. Insert needle at C to fasten.

DUPLICATE STITCH

Duplicate stitch (also known as **swiss darning**) is just that: with a blunt tapestry needle threaded with a length of yarn of a contrasting color, cover a knitted stitch with an embroidered stitch of the same shape.

BACKSTITCH

Bring needle out at A, down at B, and out again at C. Point C now becomes the point A of the next stitch.

FRENCH KNOT

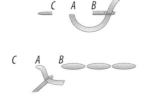

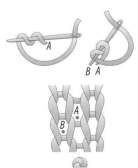

116

I-CORD

Make a tiny tube of stockinette stitch with 2 double-pointed needles:

1 Cast on 3 or 4 stitches.
2 Knit. Do not turn work. Slide stitches to opposite end of needle. Repeat Step 2 until cord is the desired length.

ATTACHED I-CORD

1 With dpn, cast on 3 or 4 stitches, then pick up and knit 1 stitch along edge of piece—4 or 5 stitches.
2 Slide stitches to opposite end of dpn and k2 or k3, then k2tog through the back loops, pick up and k 1 stitch from edge. Rep Step 2 for I-cord.

TASSELS

1 Wrap yarn around a piece of cardboard that is the desired length of the tassel. Thread a strand of yarn under the wraps, and tie it at the top, leaving a long end.

2 Cut the wrapped yarn at lower edge. Wrap the long end of yarn around upper edge and thread the yarn through the top as shown. Trim strands.

ZIPPERS

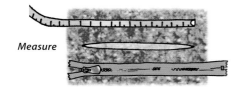

Measure

Sewing a zipper into a knit can seem daunting to the uninitiated. Although the knitted fabric has stretch, the zipper does not, and the two must be joined as neatly as possible to prevent ripples. Follow these steps for a smooth installation.

1 Measure the length of the opening. Select a zipper the length of the opening in the color of your choice. If you can't find that exact length, choose one that is a bit longer.
2 Pre-shrink your zipper in the method you will use to clean the garment. Wash and dry it or carefully steam it (you don't want to melt the teeth if they are plastic or nylon).
3 Place the zipper in opening, aligning each side. Allow extra length to extend at lower end.
4 Pin in place. Be generous with the pins, and take all the time you need. Extra care taken here makes the next steps easier.
5 Baste in place. When you are satisfied with the placement, remove the pins.
6 Sew in the zipper, making neat, even stitches that are firm enough to withstand use.
7 Sew a stop at end of zipper and clip excess off if necessary.

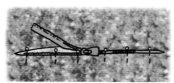

Pin

Baste

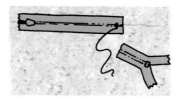

Secure stop and clip

Sew in

POMPONS

1 Cut 2 pieces of cardboard half the desired width of the pompon.
2 Place a length of yarn between cardboard pieces.
3 Hold the pieces together and wrap yarn around them.

4 Tie the length of yarn tightly at one edge.
5 Cut the wrapped yarn on opposite side.

6 Remove cardboard, fluff, and trim pompon.
7 Use ties to attach.

Pattern Specifications

INTERMEDIATE

Newborn (3, 6, 12) months
A • 18½ (21, 22, 23½)"
B • 8 (10, 11½, 13)"
C • 11½ (13¼, 14, 15)"

Skill level
Size
  and measurements

10cm/4"

27   21

• over stockinette stitch
(knit on RS, purl on WS)

Gauge
  The number of stitches and
  rows you need in 10 cm/4",
  worked as specified.

1 2 3 **4** 5 6

• Medium weight
MC, A, B, C, D, E, F • 88 yds each

Yarn weight
  and amount in yards

• 4.5mm/US 7, or size to obtain gauge

Type of needles
  Straight, unless circular
  or double-pointed
  are recommended.

• five 19mm/¾"

Buttons
  amount and size

 &

• stitch marker
• yarn needle

Any extras

Fit

C
B   A
STANDARD FIT

chest
plus 2–4"

C
B   A
LOOSE FIT

chest
plus 4–6"

C
B   A
OVERSIZED FIT

chest
plus 6" or more

Sizing

Measure around the fullest part of the chest.

Babies/Children	3 mo	6mo	12mo	18mo	24mo	2	4
Actual chest	16"	17"	18"	19"	20"	21"	23"

	Premie	Baby	Toddler
Head circumference	12"	14"	16"

Equivalent weights

¾	oz		20 g
1	oz		28 g
1½	oz		40 g
1¾	oz		50 g
2	oz		60 g
3½	oz		100 g

At a Glance

Conversion chart

centimeters		0.394	inches
grams		0.035	ounces
inches	X	2.54	centimeters
ounces		28.6	grams
meters		1.1	yards
yards		.91	meters

Needles/Hooks

US	MM	HOOK
0	2	A
1	2.25	B
2	2.75	C
3	3.25	D
4	3.5	E
5	3.75	F
6	4	G
7	4.5	7
8	5	H
9	5.5	I
10	6	J
10½	6.5	K
11	8	L
13	9	M
15	10	N
17	12.75	

Yarn weight categories

Yarn Weight

1	2	3	4	5	6
Super Fine	**Fine**	**Light**	**Medium**	**Bulky**	**Super Bulky**

Also called

Sock	Sport	DK	Worsted	Chunky	Bulky
Fingering	Baby	Light-	Afghan	Craft	Roving
Baby		Worsted	Aran	Rug	

Stockinette Stitch Gauge Range 10cm/4 inches

27 sts	23 sts	21 sts	16 sts	12 sts	6 sts
to	to	to	to	to	to
32 sts	26 sts	24 sts	20 sts	15 sts	11 sts

Recommended needle (metric)

2.25 mm	3.25 mm	3.75 mm	4.5 mm	5.5 mm	8 mm
to	to	to	to	to	and
3.25 mm	3.75 mm	4.5 mm	5.5 mm	8 mm	larger

Recommended needle (US)

1 to 3	3 to 5	5 to 7	7 to 9	9 to 11	11 and larger

Yarn substitutions

Throughout this book, the photo caption describes the yarns and colors in the photograph. If a yarn is not available, its yardage and content information will help in making a substitution. Locate the Yarn Weight and Stockinette Stitch Gauge Range over 10cm/4" on the chart. Compare that range with the information on the yarn label to find an appropriate yarn. These are guidelines only for commonly used gauges and needle sizes in specific yarn categories.

Contributors -

Harriet Adams

Nancy Bush

Lily M Chin

Kim Dolce

Susan Z. Douglas

Rosemary Drysdale

Fiona Ellis

Mary Gildersleeve

Stephanie Gildersleeve

Judith Goodman Johnson

Katharine Hunt

Mags Kandis

Wendy Keele

Irene Kubilius

Paula Levy

Michele Maks

Lorna Miser

Debbie New

Merike Saarniit

Wendy Sacks

Diane Soucy

Vicki Square

Shawn Stoner

Lizbeth Upitis

Diane Zangl